Study Guide
and Working Papers

SURVEY OF
ACCOUNTING

Study Guide and Working Papers

SURVEY OF ACCOUNTING

Katherene Terrell
Robert Terrell

Barbara Parrish
University of Central Oklahoma

David Verduzco
University of Texas, Austin

PEARSON
Prentice Hall

Upper Saddle River, New Jersey 07458

VP/Editorial Director: Jeff Shelstad
Acquisitions Editor: Bill Larkin
Assistant Editor: Sam Goffinet
Manager, Print Production: Christy Mahon
Production Editor & Buyer: Wanda Rockwell
Printer/Binder: Courier, Bookmart Press

10 9 8 7 6 5 4 3 2 1
ISBN 0-13-140921-2

Table of Contents

Preface

This *Study Guide* offers additional opportunities for study and practice on the concepts in *Survey of Accounting: Making Sense of Business,* by Katherene P. Terrell and Robert Terrell. The *Study Guide* provides a review for each of the thirteen chapters in the book, an alphabetical listing of key words introduced in each chapter, and additional application practice in various formats.

The chapter review includes the learning objective addressed in each section of the summaries. Offset by text boxes, the objectives help the student remember the important points of the materials being studied. The learning objectives identify the valuable material the authors want the student to remember.

In the applications portion of each chapter's material, the student will find study tools, including multiple-choice questions, true/false questions, matching problems, exercises, and problems to completely review the material and provide additional practice in application of the important concepts.

Solutions included in the *Study Guide* give the student immediate feedback to check the understanding of the material, from the multiple-choice questions through the problems. Working papers at the end of the *Study Guide* may be duplicated as needed by the student to use in exercises and problems in Chapters 5 and 6.

Each chapter builds on preceding ones. Therefore, each student should attain a good level of understanding of each chapter in order to better understand the following chapters.

Good luck to you in your study of the exciting field of accounting.

Chapter 1
The Business Environment

CHAPTER SUMMARY

Businesses today are highly diversified. This diversification may be in terms of markets, from local to international, or sales venues, from the traditional physically located business to Internet sales. Regardless of this diversity, however, all have the need for **relevant, reliable information** to operate effectively. The information must be functional for all types of business environments, for all types of business activities, for all forms of ownership, for multiple relationships, and for the expanded marketplace. At the same time, the information must possess integrity and adhere to high standards of accuracy.

LO 1: Define business activity and the profit motive.

Business has the specific function of providing demanded products and services to those who desire them. The motivation for most business owners to undertake the activity comes from the goal of creating a **profit** for the owner(s). Not all individuals require that their efforts return tangible rewards; some businesses are characterized as **not-for-profit**. The rewards of those involved in these enterprises derive from the satisfaction of meeting the needs of those individuals served.

In order to support economic activity, four factors of production are utilized. **Entrepreneurial efforts** bring together needed **natural resources**, **human resources**, and **physical capital** to create a business and direct it toward the desired goal. Accomplishment of the goal requires that the entrepreneurs know the direction the business must take. A **business plan**, therefore, specifies the direction of the business and sets forth the procedures anticipated for accomplishing business goals.

LO 2: Distinguish among the three major types of business activities and hybrid businesses.

The business activity itself may be classified according to the manner in which it serves its audience. Businesses may be primarily **(1) manufacturing, (2) merchandising**—either **retail** or **wholesale**--, or **(3) service**. Of course, any given business may have characteristics of more than one of these classifications and be a **hybrid** business .

LO 3 : Distinguish among the three basic forms of business organizations and describe the advantages and disadvantages of each.

The business form selected by the owners depends on the owner (s) views of the advantages and disadvantages of each form. Primarily, three forms differ in terms of their basic characteristics. **(1) Sole proprietorships, (2) partnerships**, and **(3) corporations** possess distinct qualities which makes them more attractive (or less attractive) to specific businesspeople

1

The Business Environment

than the other forms. Additionally, some of the qualities of partnerships and corporations have been altered by newly formulated types of business forms. The advantages and disadvantages of each form, as they relate to the preferences of the business owner(s), drive the choice of form for the business. The table below summarizes these advantages and disadvantages.

Advantages	Disadvantages
Sole Proprietorship	
One owner	Unlimited liability
Not legally separate	Limited access to capital
Easy and inexpensive to start	Limited access to expertise
Total control	Huge time commitment
No separate tax	
Partnership	
Easy formation	Unlimited liability
Utilization of complementary skills	Problems with withdrawal of partner
Improved access to capital	Sharing of profits
No separate taxation	May encounter conflicts
	Ability of one partner to obligate others (mutual agency)
Corporation	
Greater capital	Double taxation
Limited liability	More governmental oversight
Professional management	
Unlimited life	

LO 4: Identify the stakeholders of a business and describe social responsibility.

Business relationships have become much more complex in recent years. An additional responsibility of businesses lies in awareness of the stakeholders of the business. **Stakeholders** may include **customers, employees, stockholders,** and **competitors**, as well as the **government and the community.** All business owners must consider the impact of decisions on affected stakeholders, whether required by law or as a result of ethical considerations. Maintaining a balance among these concerned entities requires businesses to examine all aspects of decisions being made. The emphasis on being a good citizen has been expanded for businesses.

LO 5: Identify the attributes and evaluate the importance of business reputation and ethical behavior.

Most businesses take their responsibility for being good citizens seriously and work hard to build a successful reputation. Qualities necessary for building these reputations include **an enduring corporate culture, product and service quality, innovation, financial strength, attraction and retention of talented people, and social responsibility.**

LO 6: Compare and contrast the relationships between a business and its employees, other businesses, consumers, and government.

To operate successfully in today's environment, businesses need to maintain a high business reputation and ethical standards. **Employees** reflect the behavior indicated by the corporate culture. They want fairness, ethics, and equity along with additional specialized workplace perquisites. **Other businesses** to which an entity sells will want to deal with trustworthy companies and to be trustworthy. **Consumers**, too, will evaluate a company on the relationship between costs and benefits. Businesses will also sell to **government** agencies by which the businesses are evaluated.

LO 7: Discuss the effect of e-commerce on business practices.

Those businesses which deal in e-commerce find the characteristics of that type of business to be conducive to generating higher approval ratings from customers. Because communication time is dramatically reduced, costs can be lowered and monetary savings can be dramatic. The continuing nature of the sales venue allows faster processing of payments and closer contact with customers. The closer contact can be utilized to generate improved customer service.

LO 8: Define accounting and distinguish among the different roles of accountants.

In this complex business environment, the accounting system provides useful information to all types of decision makers. These decision makers may be within the organization, such as management or the board of directors, (internal decision makers) or outside the organization, such as stockholders, creditors, regulatory or government agents, and investors, (external decision makers). Accountants provide two types of accounting information. Financial accounting information provides historical financial information to both internal and external decision makers in a specified format. Management accounting conveys both financial and non-financial information to internal decision makers.

The accounting profession itself began its evolution after the stock market crash of 1929. As a reaction to deficiencies in financial information provided to investors, Congress enacted the Securities Acts of 1933 and 1934. The 1934 Act created the Securities and Exchange Commission (SEC) to monitor the markets. Though it possesses the authority to establish accounting principles, the SEC has delegated that authority to the accounting profession. As a result, the current standards-issuing body is the Financial Accounting Standards Board (FASB). The authority of the SEC extends only to those companies that are publicly traded, and those companies are the ones which must utilize the accounting rules issued by the FASB. Recently, the International Accounting Standards Board has come into existence and is issuing standards and rules for statement presentation internationally.

Recently, in reaction to the failures of some large companies, Congress has enacted the Sarbanes-Oxley Act of 2002 which imposes strict penalties for reporting errors and fraudulent financial statements. The Accounting Oversight Board has the responsibility of overseeing both the accounting profession and the SEC.

Accountants who meet educational and professional criteria to be licensed by a state board of accountancy and who have passed the examination are called Certified Public Accountants. These individuals are required to adhere to strict ethical standards. The ethical failures of the early 2000's resulted from the actions of a few individuals who did not follow the required standards.

Accountants provide assurance services for clients, including attestation, auditing of financial statements, and internal control evaluation. They also assist companies in taxation, consulting, and management accounting.

CHAPTER GLOSSARY

Accountant: an information specialist who provides a variety of accounting and consultation services to businesses and individuals

Accounting: a system for analyzing and recording business transactions, transforming the resulting data into information useful for decision making, and reporting to the proper stakeholders

Assurance services: independent professional services that improve the quality of information, or its context, for decision makers

Attestation: involves the evaluation of one party's assertion to a third party

Auditing: a process of gathering objective evidence, evaluating the evidence against specific criteria, and reporting the results to the users of the information

Board of directors: a group of people who have ultimate responsibility for managing the corporation

Business: the process of producing and distributing goods and services to those who desire them. Also commonly used to refer to individual companies.

Business plan: details of a firm's business goals and its action plan to achieve those goals

Certified Public Accountant: an individual who meets educational and professional criteria to be licensed by a state board of accountancy

Chief financial officer: a person who directs the firm's financial affairs

Consulting services: activities in which an accountant provides data, decision information, and other advice that helps the client manage the business

Corporate culture: an organization's values and beliefs

Corporation: a separate legal entity with the rights and obligations of a person

Cost accounting: a narrow application of management accounting dealing specifically with procedures designed to determine how much a particular item (usually a unit of manufactured product) costs

Dividend: a distribution of part of the firm's after-tax profit to the shareholders

E-commerce: business transactions that are conducted electronically through the Internet and other electronic media

Entrepreneurship: creativity, willingness to accept risk, and management skills necessary to combine natural resources, human resources, and physical capital into business activity

Ethics: a system of standards of conduct and moral judgment

External decision makers: people outside the company who made decisions *about* the company from limited information furnished by the entity's management

Factors of production: the four major items needed to support economic activity.

Final consumer: the final user of a product

Financial accounting: provides historical financial information to internal and external decision makers

Financial Accounting Standards Board: the organization principally responsible for establishing accounting guidelines and rules, in the United States, at the present time

Financial statement audit: an examination by an independent CPA of enough of a company's records to determine whether the financial statements were prepared in accordance with GAAP and demonstrate a fair representation of the company's financial condition

Generally accepted accounting principles: guidelines for presentation of financial accounting information designed to serve external decision makers' need for consistent and comparable information

Human resources: mental and physical efforts of all workers who produce the goods and services for a society

Hybrid company: a company that participates significantly in more than one type of business activity

Independence: a requirement that an accountant has no personal or financial interest (direct or indirect) in the client being examined

Internal control structure: a process designed to provide assurance that an entity can report reliable financial information, comply with laws and regulations, operate efficiently and effectively, and safeguard its assets

Internal decision makers: people within the organization who make decisions *for* the company and have almost unlimited access to accounting information

International Accounting Standards Board: an independent organization responsible for establishing international accounting standards and rules of statement presentation

Limited liability company: a corporation in which stockholders enjoy the limited liability status of a corporation but are taxed as partners in a partnership

Limited liability partnership: a partnership that limits the liability of a general partner to his or her own negligence or misconduct or the behavior of persons he or she controls

Limited partnership: a partnership that consists of at least one general partner and one or more limited partners

Management accounting: provides detailed financial information and non-financial information to internal decision makers

Manufacturing: the business activity that converts raw materials into a tangible, physical product

Merchandising: the business activity of selling finished goods produced by other companies

Monopolistic practices: Taking advantage of consumers by raising prices unfairly because a business is the main supplier of a particular good or service

Natural resources: include air currents, water, land, and things that come from the earth such as timber, minerals, oil, and natural gas

Not-for-profit firms: generally benevolent organizations formed to serve the needs of society instead of earning profits to distribute to owners

Partnership: a business with two or more owners who all share in the risks and profits of the entity

Physical capital: buildings, equipment, tools, and infrastructure required to produce goods and services

Predatory pricing: marking prices so low that competitors are forced to drop out of the market because they cannot remain profitable

Price discrimination: charging different prices to different customers to lessen competition

Price fixing: a group of competitors agree to set a uniform market price to increase their profits

Profit: the excess of revenues over expenses (Revenue minus expenses = profit)

Securities and Exchange Commission: the government agency empowered by Congress to regulate securities sales and establish accounting rules, standards, procedures, and the form of published financial reporting

Separate entity assumption: the assumption that economic activity can be identified with a particular economic entity and that the results of the activities will be separately recorded

Service: a business activity that provides specific work or a job function as its major operation

Social responsibility: attitudes and actions that exhibit sensitivity to social and environmental concerns

Sole proprietorship: a business that is owned by a single individual and is not legally separate from the owner

Stakeholder: any person or entity affected by the way a company conducts its business

Stock: certificates of ownership in a corporation

Stockholder: a person or entity who owns shares of stock in a corporation and has the right to vote on how to operate the business and receive profit distributions. Also called a shareholder.

PROBLEM APPLICATIONS

Multiple Choice Questions:

For each of the following multiple choice questions, circle the letter of the BEST response.

1. Which of the following factors of production is vital to all types of business activity?
    A. Natural resources
    B. Human resources
    C. Physical capital
    D. Entrepreneurship

2. A manufacturing firm must
    A. always sell directly to the consumer
    B. never sell directly to the consumer
    C. start the manufacturing process with unprocessed natural resources
    D. convert an input into a different output product

2. Which of the following businesses would be considered a merchandising operation?
    A. Hospital
    B. Hardware store
    C. Accounting partnership
    D. Restaurant

3. Which of the following is an advantage of the corporate form of business?
    A. Unlimited liability
    B. Life independent of the owners
    C. Double taxation
    D. Lack of interference by stockholders

4. The largest number of business organizations in the United States is
    A. Corporations.
    B. Limited liability companies.
    C. Partnerships.
    D. Sole proprietorships

5. The type of business organization in the United States which has the most capital is
    A. Corporations.
    B. Limited liability companies.
    C. Partnerships.
    D. Sole proprietorships.

6. Which of the following groups would be considered internal decision makers?
   A. Customers.
   B. Competitors.
   C. Government.
   D. Employees.

7. The use of e-commerce usually
   A.   reduces the time required to complete a business transaction
   B.   requires additional staff to make sure transactions are handled quickly.
   C.   increases the cost of business transactions
   D.   increases costs for people who don't have computers.

8. Financial accounting provides information
   A. only to internal decision makers.
   B. only to external decision makers.
   C. in a specialized format.
   D. regarding the manner in which decisions were made.

9. Which organization is actually responsible for establishing accounting principles?
   A. Securities and Exchange Commission (SEC).
   B. Financial Accounting Standards Board (FASB).
   C. American Institute of Certified Public Accountants (AICPA)
   D. None of the above.

10. An advantage of conducting business with other businesses is that
    A. you can learn more about the other business in order to compete with it.
    B. not having to charge sales tax saves record keeping.
    C. advertising costs are lessened.
    D. the other business will often provide gifts for you.

11. An advantage of conducting business by e-commerce is that
    A. customer complaints are avoided.
    B. customers are more willing to give you information.
    C. collections are faster.
    D. you don't have the pressure to deliver by a specific date.

12. Independence is a requirement that an accountant has
    A. no financial interests in the client being examined
    B. no personal interests in the client being examined.
    C. no personal or financial interests in the client being examined.
    D. no knowledge of the client being examined.

13. The Sarbanes-Oxley Act of 2002 was passed to
    A. create new accounting rules.
    B. increase penalties for management and auditors for reporting errors.
    C. eliminate the SEC.
    D. eliminate accountant's self monitoring.

14. The internal control structure of a firm
    A. allows the auditor to determine a comfort level with the system.
    B. provides assurance that the numbers are correct.
    C. prevents fraud and theft from the company.
    D. indicates areas the auditor needs to fix.

15. The Chief Financial Officer of a company
    A. oversees all operations.
    B. must be a CPA.
    C. makes all decisions on capital purchases.
    D. is concerned with both managerial and financial accounting.

True / False Questions:

Indicate whether each of the following statements is true (T) or false (F). If a statement is false, note the part of the statement which makes it false.

_____ 1. All organizations are formed to earn profits.
_____ 2. Physical capital might include buildings, equipment, and tools.
_____ 3. A merchandising company converts raw materials into a tangible, physical product.
_____ 4. Because a sole proprietorship is legally an extension of its owner, all business obligations become the owner's legal obligations.
_____ 5. Predatory pricing is an effective means of being competitive.
_____ 6. All employees, from shipping clerks to the president, affect how the organization functions and services its customers.
_____ 7. Governments are among the largest consumers of products and services offered by businesses.
_____ 8. All companies are required to follow generally accepted accounting principles.
_____ 9. Attestation involves the evaluation of one party's assertion to a third party.
_____ 10. The chief accounting officer directs a company's financial affairs.
_____ 11. A wholesale merchandising firm can also be a retail merchandising firm.

Matching:

Listed below are the forms of business in the United States:

a.   Sole proprietorship   d.   Partnership
b.   Limited partnership   e.   Limited liability partnership
c.   Corporation   f.   Limited liability company

For each of the characteristics below, identify all forms to which the trait applies.

1.   _____double taxation   2.   _____two or more owners
3.   _____only one owner   4.   _____pays dividends
5.   _____separate entity (accounting) 6.   _____combination of limited and
                                                   general partners
7.   _____some owners precluded from   8.   _____limits on liability of owners
          decision making   9.   _____owners active in business
10. _____high time commitment   11. _____ease of generating capital
12. _____greater access to special skills 13. _____lack of continuity
14. _____unlimited life   15. _____elimination of conflict
16. _____no separate taxes   17. _____complete owner control

Exercises:

1.   Identify the full name for which the following acronyms are used:
     a.   CPA   b.   CFO
     c.   FASB   d.   LLC
     e.   LLP   f.   SEC
     g.   NAICS   h.   GAAP
     i.   IASB

2.   International Business Machines Corporation (IBM) uses information technology to provide customer solutions that include technologies, systems, products, services, software and financing. What type of business activity is being performed by the company?

3.   The Dow Chemical Company is a science and technology company that provides chemical, plastic and agricultural products and services to consumer markets. Describe the manner in which customers, employees, stockholders, and the community want the company to provide for them.

4.   Dell, Inc. designs, manufactures, markets, and services computer systems, including desktop, notebooks and enterprise systems. The company also markets software, peripherals, service, and support programs. How might the company use e-commerce in its operations?

5.　　Dell, Inc. designs, manufactures, markets, and services computer systems, including desktop, notebooks and enterprise systems. The company also markets software, peripherals, service, and support programs. How might the company's use of e-commerce affect the company's profits.

SOLUTIONS

Multiple Choice:

1. D
2. D
3. B
4. D
5. A
6. D
7. A
8. C
9. B
10. C
11. C
12. C
13. B
14. A
15. D

True / False:

1. False; not-for-profit firms are generally formed to serve the needs of society.
2. True
3. False; a *manufacturing* company converts raw materials into a tangible, physical product.
4. True
5. False; trade laws require that a company not engage in predatory pricing.
6. True
7. True
8. False; only companies regulated by the SEC are legally required to follow GAAP.
9. True
10. False; the chief *financial* officer directs company's financial affairs.
11. True.

Matching:

1	C	11.	C
2	B, C, D, E, F	12.	B, C, D, E., F
3	A	13.	A, B, D, E, F
4	C	14.	C
5	A, B, C, D, E, F	15.	NONE
6	B	16.	A, B, D, E, F
7	B, E	17.	A
8	B, C, E, F		
9	A, B, C, D, E, F		
10	A		

Exercises:

1. a.   Certified Public Accountant
    b.   Corporate Financial Officer
    c.   Financial Accounting Standards Board
    d.   Limited Liability Company
    e.   Limited Liability Partnership
    f.   Securities and Exchange Commission
    g.   North American Industrial Classification System
    h.   Generally Accepted Accounting Principles
    i.   International Accounting Standards Board

2. The company would be considered a hybrid company since it provides a variety of products and services.

3. Customers would want quality products that would pose no serious health or safety risks. Employees would want fair wages and employment opportunities as well as safe working conditions. Stockholders would want the value of their investment to grow. The community in which the company operates would want the company to produce its products with no harm to the environment.

4. The company would likely sell its products and services over the internet. They may also communicate and integrate their systems with suppliers through some form of electronic media to improve the flow of goods. The company may also provide customers with account, order status and billing information through electronic means.

5. The use of e-commerce would allow the company to reduce or eliminate the need and cost of retail space as well as paper and postage costs to communicate with suppliers and customers. A reduction of costs would increase the company's profits.

Chapter 2
Basic Concepts of Accounting
and Financial Reporting

CHAPTER SUMMARY

When FASB was organized, a primary consideration was to develop a conceptual framework to define accounting theory and to guide board members in developing accounting rules. Starting with the **objectives of financial reporting**, the project participants next developed a set of **qualitative characteristics** which should be present in accounting information. The information was to be conveyed through the **accounting elements**, subject to specified **principles, assumptions, and constraints.** These ideas have served the accounting profession for approximately 30 years and provide a cohesive set of guidelines for those individuals involved in developing GAAP. An understanding of these guidelines allows the student of accounting to more completely comprehend the care applied in developing accounting rules.

LO 1: Describe the objectives of accounting and useful accounting information.

The accountant must take the **accounting data** generated in daily business operations and convert it to meaningful **accounting information** to be used by economic decision makers. The information, in order to be meaningful, must be useful in specific ways by these decision makers. The information **must be useful to decision makers in (1) making investment, credit, and other important business decisions, (2) assessing certainty, timing, and amounts of future cash flows, and (3) understanding about the entity's resources, claims against those resources, and changes in the resources and claims over time.** The ability of the information to meet these objectives for the user is **subject to the user's reasonable level of understanding and knowledge about the accounting rules and presentation.**

LO 2: Define the qualitative characteristics of accounting information and determine the effect of each on information.

Having determined the manner in which accounting information must provide benefits to financial statement users, FASB next identified the **qualitative characteristics** of the information which would allow it to be useful. The **primary qualitative characteristics** are **relevance** and **reliability**. A problem faced by the accountant is that these characteristics occur at vastly different times and must, therefore, be balanced in some manner. **Relevance** refers to the most recent information. **Timeliness** is required; otherwise, the information will arrive too late to help in making decisions. Relevant information also possesses **predictive value** so that it can be used to assess future performance of the company. Relevant information also must have **feedback value** so that it can be used to evaluate past predictions about the company.

Reliability, on the other hand, describes the ability of information to be dependable. This characteristic becomes present with the passage of time. The more time has passed, the more we know about the correctness of information we possess. To be reliable, information must possess **verifiability** so that various qualified individuals would reach similar conclusions when they examine it. Reliable information also possesses **representational faithfulness**; it really shows the event it is describes. Lastly, reliable information must be characterized by **neutrality.** It should just present the facts without any attempt to influence the financial statement user.

In addition to the primary characteristics of relevance and reliability, accounting information must also possess the secondary characteristics of **comparability** and **consistency.** While these characteristics sound similar, they have different meanings in accounting. **Comparability** allows users of financial statements to examine the similarities and differences of various companies' financial information. This characteristic allows the financial statement user to make decisions regarding the relationships between companies. Alternatively, **consistency** relates to the information of one company across time. The company should follow the same accounting rules, applied in the same manner, so that the results presented show a true picture of the increases and decreases of various items.

LO 3: Define the elements o' accounting and construct the accounting equation.

The accounting system conveys the information through the use of ten **accounting elements** which are used to construct four financial statements. These ten elements are **assets, liabilities, equity, investments by owners, distributions to owners, revenues, expenses, gains, losses, and comprehensive income.** The first three elements comprise the basis of the double-entry accounting system. The accounting equation states that **assets = liabilities + equity.** This statement requires that all items of value in a company must eventually be used to either satisfy debts of the company or returned to the owners of the company. The equation also describes the content of the balance sheet, one of the four financial statements.

LO 4: Recognize a balance sheet, income statement, statement of equity, and statement of cash flows and determine which accounting elements comprise each statement.

The **balance sheet** presents the **assets, liabilities,** and **equity** of the company and shows the position of the company at a specific date in time. It lists all assets held by the company and demonstrates the assets' equality with the total liabilities and total equity. The equity may be "contributed" by the owners in exchange for an ownership share in the company. Equity may also be earned by the company through profitable operations and by retaining the results of these operations in the company.

The balance sheet of a company differs from other types of financial statements and among types of businesses. Only the balance sheet of a business presents information **as of a specific point in time**. The date on a balance sheet shows the one date on which the information existed. All other financial statements cover a period of time. Additionally, only the balance sheet shows any differences among types of businesses. In the equity section, sole proprietorships and partnerships use owner(s)' name(s) associated with capital accounts to record the owner(s)' investments in the company. Corporations, however, have a stock account, usually Common Stock, and a Retained Earnings account. The stock account maintains information on the original investments by owners while the Retained Earnings account records all earnings of the company that have been kept (retained) by the company. Earnings of the company are computed on a second financial statement called the Income Statement.

An **income statement** measures earnings of the company for a specified period of time, often a quarter (three months) or a year. The elements shown on the income statement include **revenues, expenses, gains, and losses**. Revenues and gains are inflows (rewards) to the company while expenses and losses (sacrifices) are outflows. Inflows in excess of outflows leads to **net income** while outflows in excess of inflows creates a **net loss**. The income statement, like the balance sheet, uses a formula to compute and present the accounting information.

In creating the income statement, an accountant first measures revenues (inflows from business activity) for the company. These revenues may come from sales of merchandise or sales of services to the customer. If the revenues come from sales of merchandise, a form of expense called **cost of goods sold** is associated with the merchandise sale. This expense represents the cost of the items sold while the revenue represents the selling price of the merchandise sold. **Gross profit** results from taking the revenues (sales) amount minus the cost of goods sold. **Operating expenses**, those additional costs of running the business, are deducted from gross profit to determine **operating income**. Operating income describes the net inflows from the primary activity of the business. Because businesses encounter inflows and outflows outside the primary activities, the next section on the income statement shows **other revenue and expenses**. This category may also include gains and losses. Because corporations must pay taxes like individuals do, the **income tax expense** is deducted next to arrive at **net income**.

The next statement provided by corporations is the **statement of stockholders' equity**. This statement updates the equity accounts to end-of-the-period balances and provides information to the financial statement users regarding the causes of changes in the account balances. Additional **investments by owners** during the period are added to the stock accounts. In some cases, **comprehensive income** shows increases to the retained earnings account. In many cases, through, the only increase to retained earnings derives from the net income reported on the income statement. Reductions in the retained earnings account occur from net losses from operations and from distributions to owners. These distributions are called **dividends** in a corporation. Comprehensive income and dividends complete our listing of the accounting elements set forth by FASB.

The last of the financial statements provided by companies is the **statement of cash flows**. This statement serves to highlight the vital need for a company to monitor its cash. Without more cash coming into the business than going out, the business cannot continue to exist. The statement builds on the three primary functions of a business—operating, investing, and financing activities. The daily activities of a business, those which are recorded on the income statement, are operating activities. Investing activities focus on those investments made by the company, and financing activities encompass the manner in which the company generates cash to start and continue the business. The complete statement of cash flows explains the items that have increased and decreased the cash account during the period of the statement.

The ties among the statements is called **articulation**. The income statement's net income or net loss appears as an adjustment to the owners' equity (the retained earnings account in a corporation). Updated equity balances flow to the balance sheet, and the statement of cash flows indicates the causes of cash account changes. Taken together, the statements provide a complete and cohesive view of the activities of the company for the period(s) covered by the statements.

LO 5: Identify the underlying assumptions of accounting and describe how they affect financial reporting.

In recording and reporting the company's activities, accountants make some assumptions which must be understood by the financial statement users. These assumptions influence the choices made in recording and presenting the accounting information each period. The first of these is the **separate entity assumption**. This assumption allows the separation of business activities from the activities of the owner(s). A business is viewed as a separate entity which can enter into transactions.

A second assumption is the **going concern assumption**. Without evidence to the contrary, a business is assumed to be continuing for an indefinite period into the future. This assumption permits accountants to allow the business to hold assets and to owe liabilities.

The **monetary unit assumption** states that business activities can be measured and expressed in terms of the currency in use. This assumption ignores inflation and deflation. The rapid changes occurring in businesses and the stability of the monetary unit have generally allowed accounting to use this assumption without problems.

Last, accounting utilizes the **periodicity assumption**. This assumption says that accountants can arbitrarily divide the life of the business into periods of a year or less for purposes of reporting to investors, government, and taxing authorities. Without this assumption, financial statement users would not have accounting information in a timely manner. The requirement of periodic reporting provides much more meaningful information than would otherwise be available.

LO 6: Define the underlying principles of accounting and describe how they affect financial reporting.

In addition to the assumptions used in accounting, four principles guide accountants in making decisions about when and how to record information. The **historical cost principle** requires that amounts on the balance sheet be recorded at acquisition cost, not current value. These items will generally remain at historical cost regardless of the period they are held by the company. Historical cost provides an objective and verifiable measurement amount and is not subject to differences in opinions by various authorities.

A second principle, **revenue recognition**, provides guidance for the accountant on when revenue should be recorded on the accounting records. When the revenue has been earned and an enforceable claim exists to receive an asset of value, the accountant can recognize (record) the transaction. Earned revenues usually generate either an inflow of cash or a promise to pay in the future, a promise called an Account Receivable.

Tied to the revenue recognition principle, the **matching principle** states that expenses relate to revenues recognized in a specific period and this association triggers the recording of the expense. **Matching** can be accomplished in several ways. Most directly, accountants may establish a direct cause and effect relationship between the revenues and the expenses. The best example of a cause and effect lies in the sales revenue being coupled with cost of goods sold. These two values relate to identical items. Absent such direct coupling, however, accountants may simply recognize expenses as they are incurred or may spread (allocate) a cost over the future periods which benefit from its incurrence. The depreciating of items such as buildings or cars over the periods in which they are used provides one of the best-known examples of an allocation.

Finally, the **full disclosure principle** states than any information needed by a knowledgeable user of financial statements to make an economic decision regarding the company should be made available. The information may appear in the financial statements themselves or in the footnotes which follow, but it must be available.

> **LO 7: Identify the underlying constraints of accounting and describe how they affect accounting decisions and reporting.**

The last qualities that define accounting information are the constraints accountants apply. The **materiality constraint** identifies a threshhold consideration. An item is considered material if it is large enough to make a difference in the decision of a knowledgeable person. An immaterial item may be ignored or handled in a somewhat different manner than would otherwise be required.

Cost-benefit requires that the benefit of the information should be greater than the cost of generating it. This measure relates to benefit to the user versus cost to the company supplying that information. These measures obviously may be difficult to determine and compare.

As a result of the desire to not mislead the financial statement user in cases where exact numbers cannot be determined, the **conservatism constraint** guides the accountant's choices. The numbers presented to financial statement users should be those which tend toward understating assets and overstating liabilities. Making choices in this manner protects the company from leading the financial statement user to believe the company is worth more than it truly is.

Last, **industry practices** lead to differences in financial statement treatment for certain specialized industries. For example, oil and gas explorers have special rules as do financial instititions. These practices must be followed in the specified areas but are not applicable to most companies.

The entire **conceptual framework** provides guidance to those who make accounting rules, and knowledge of these ideas assist users of financial statements in understanding the meaning of the items shown in the financial statements and disclosed in the notes following the statements. A complete understanding of accounting requires incorporation of the ideas provided by the conceptual framework.

CHAPTER GLOSSARY

Account receivable: a customer's legal promise to pay cash in the future

Accounting data: the raw results of economic transactions and events

Accounting equation: assets equal liabilities plus equity

Accounting information: the product of accountants' organization, classification, and summary of economic transactions and events so that it is useful to economic decision makers

Articulation: the linkage between the financial statements

Assets: things an entity owns or controls that have future value

Balance sheet: the financial statement that provides information about the present condition of a business at a specific point in time. A balance sheet consists of three accounting elements: assets, liabilities, and equity

Comparability: the quality of information that allows users to identify similarities in and differences between two sets of accounting information

Comprehensive income: the change in equity arising from any non-owner source

Conservatism: choosing alternatives that are least likely to overstate assets and income or understate liabilities when uncertainty or doubt exists

Consistency: conformity from period to period with accounting policies and procedures

Cost of goods sold: the cost of merchandise transferred to a customer in the entity's primary business activity

Cost-benefit relationship: the benefit of knowing information should exceed the cost of providing information

Depreciation: the allocation of the cost of long-lived assets to the periods benefited by its use

Distributions to owners: transfers of cash or other company assets to owners that result in a reduction of equity

Earned equity: the total amount a company has earned since its beginning, less any amounts distributed to its owner(s)

Equity: the difference between the entity's assets and its liabilities

Expenses: sacrifices of the future value of assets used to generate revenues from customers

Feedback value: the quality of information that allows users to substantiate or amend prior expectations

Full disclosure principle: requires that information necessary for an informed user of the financial statements of a business enterprise to make an economic decision must be made available to the statement users

Gains: increases in net assets (equity) that result from incidental or other peripheral events that affect the entity, except for normal revenues and investments by owners

Going-concern principle: in the absence of any information to the contrary, a business entity will remain in existence for an indefinite time

Gross profit: sales minus the cost of goods sold

Historical cost principle: requires that balance sheet items be reported at the total cost at acquisition instead of a current value

Income statement: a financial report that provides information about an entity's financial performance during a specific time period

Industry practices: certain industries may require departure from generally accepted accounting principles (GAAP), because of the peculiar nature of the industry or a particular transaction, to ensure fair presentation of the financial information within that industry

Information: data that are put into some useful form for decision making

Basic Concepts of Accounting and Financial Reporting

Investments by owners: represents the amount invested by the company's owner(s) to get it started or to finance its expansion

Liabilities: the obligations of an entity to transfer assets to, or perform services for, a third party

Losses: decreases in net assets (equity) that result from incidental or other peripheral events that affect the entity, except for normal expenses and distributions to owners

Matching principle: requires that a company match revenue with the expense of producing that revenue

Materiality: something that will influence the judgment of a reasonable person

Monetary unit assumption: economic activities are measured and expressed in terms of the appropriate currency for a business

Net income: the difference between the rewards (revenues and gains) and the sacrifices (expenses and losses) for a given period of activity is the net reward of doing business

Net loss: occurs when the expenses and losses for the period are greater than the revenues and gains for the period

Neutrality: absence of bias intended to influence reported information

Periodicity assumption: measurement of economic activity over an arbitrary time period, such as a year or month, for the purpose of providing useful information

Predictive value: the quality of information that assists users to increase the probability of correctly forecasting the results of past or present events

Relevance: a characteristic of useful accounting information that requires the information to pertain to and make a difference in a particular decision situation

Reliability: a characteristic of useful accounting information that requires the information to be reasonably unbiased and accurate

Representational faithfulness: validity or agreement between a measure or description and the event that it represents

Revenue recognition principle: revenue recognition occurs when the revenue is earned and an enforceable claim exists to receive the asset traded for the revenue

Revenues: increases in net assets (equity) that occur as a result of an entity's selling or producing products and performing services for its customers

Separate entity assumption: economic transactions and activities of a business can be accounted for separately and apart from the personal activities of the owners

Statement of cash flows: a financial statement that details cash provided and used by the three major functions of a firm: to operate, to invest resources, and to finance the operations and investments

Statement of stockholders' equity: the financial statement that reports the change in the entity's equity during a period of time

Timeliness: having information before it is too late to influence decisions

Verifiability: the ability of information to be substantiated by unbiased measures

PROBLEM APPLICATIONS

Multiple Choice Questions:

For each of the following multiple choice questions, circle the letter of the BEST response.

1. The accounting equation states that
   A. Assets + Liabilities = Equity
   B. Assets = Liabilities – Equity
   C. Assets + Equity = Liabilities
   D. Assets = Liabilities + Equity

2. The conceptual framework of accounting
   A. has been in existence since accounting began.
   B. provides a framework for accounting rules.
   C. was established by the Securities and Exchange Commission
   D. changes as the economy changes.

3. The objectives of financial reporting require that accounting information
   A. provide useful information to all financial statement users.
   B. provide useful information about the philosophy of the business.
   C. provide useful information for investment decisions.
   D. provide useful information for hiring decisions.

4. The primary qualitative characteristics of accounting information are
   A. relevance and reliability.
   B. consistency and comparability.
   C. objectivity and verifiability.
   D. timeliness and objectivity.

5. Relevant information needs to have
   A. timeliness and consistency.
   B. numerical value and predictive value.
   C. predictive value and feedback value.
   D. verifiability and neutrality.

6. The financial statement that expresses the accounting equation is the
   A. income statement.
   B. statement of stockholders' equity.
   C. balance sheet.
   D. statement of cash flows.

7. The two sources of equity in a business are
   A. earnings and borrowings
   B. owner investments and borrowings.
   C. earnings and dividends.
   D. earnings and owner investments.

8. The only financial statement to have a date line showing only one day is the
   A. income statement.
   B. statement of stockholders' equity.
   C. balance sheet.
   D. statement of cash flows.

9. Gains and losses appear on the
   A. income statement.
   B. statement of stockholders' equity.
   C. statement of retained earnings.
   D. balance sheet.

10. Gross profit equals
   A. assets minus liabilities.
   B. sales minus liabilities.
   C. sales minus cost of goods sold.
   D. sales minus expenses.

11 Distributions to owners are called
   A. expenses.
   B. dividends.
   C. payments.
   D. loans.

12. A cash outflow from an operating activity would include
   A. cash amounts for buying inventory.
   B. cash amounts from borrowing from a bank.
   C. cash amounts for buying equipment.
   D. cash amounts from selling equipment.

13. The historical cost principle requires that balance sheet items be reported at their
   A. cost at the time of purchase.
   B. market value at the balance sheet date.
   C. market value at the time of appraisal.
   D. index-adjusted cost at balance sheet date.

14. The going-concern assumption recognizes that
   A. economic activity should be measured over a specific time period for the purpose of providing useful information.
   B. economic activities should be measured in terms of an appropriate currency for the business.
   C. economic transactions should be accounted for separately and apart from the personal on-going activities of the owners.
   D. in the absence of any information to the contrary, a business entity will continue to remain in existence for an indefinite period of time.

15. Financial statement articulation refers to
   A. the humor in the statements.
   B. the similarities in the statements.
   C. the connections among the statements.
   D. the format of the statements.

16. In order to recognize revenue, a company must have substantially completed the terms of the sale or service which generally occurs at the time of the
   A. customer order.
   B. product manufacture.
   C. product delivery.
   D. customer payment.

17. The net income equation can be represented as
   A. Revenues – Expenses + Gains – Losses = Net Income
   B. Gains – Losses = Net Income
   C. Assets - Expenses + Gains – Losses = Net Income
   D. Assets – Liabilities = Net Income

True / False Questions:

1. The usefulness criterion of accounting information requires a user who is knowledgeable about accounting rules.
2. To be relevant, accounting information should be timely and should either assist users to correctly forecast results or to substantiate prior expectations.
3. Timeliness requires that information be available to financial statement users in time to prove or disprove the accuracy of their decisions.
4. Accounting information would be considered verifiable if several individuals working together would agree on conclusions about the data.
5. Accounting information is generally presented from the perspective of an investor.
6. Consistency refers to the need for different companies to use the same accounting policies and procedures.
7. Comparability is the quality of information that allows users to identify similarities in and differences between two sets of accounting information.
8. To be considered an asset, an item should have future value.
9. Liabilities arise from past transactions and are the obligations of an entity to transfer assets or perform services for a third party.
10. Equity must come directly from investors.
11. The accounting equation can be rearranged such that assets minus liabilities equal equity.
12. Expenses can be considered liabilities.
13. Consistency relates to companies using the same accounting procedures from year to year.
14. Gains impact the income statement in the same way revenues impact it.
15. Cost of goods sold includes advertising costs and salespeople's wages.
16. The date line on an income statement tells the financial statement user how much time the statement covers and when the time period ends.
17. Other comprehensive income must be shown in the revenue section of the income statement.
18. The Retained Earnings account represents all of the cash the company has.
19. The statement of cash flows has three sections: operating, investing, and financing.
20. Deducting the owner's daughter's college tuition is a violation of the matching principle.

Matching:

1. Identify the assumption, principle, or constraint that is violated in each case.

_____ 1. An owner uses one checking account for both his personal and business transactions and combines the information in financial statements.

_____ 2. A person in the oil business uses the rules set forth for retail businesses for his accounting.

_____ 3. Mary Lou refuses to provide information on the loans the company has outstanding at Neighborhood Bank.

_____ 4. Joe has warranties which will arise for his product. The accountant has provided him with a range of possible costs between $10,000 and $25,000, with any amount within the range being equally likely. Joe picks the $10,000 for his financial statements.

_____ 5. The owner of XYZ Enterprises has his cars appraised annually and records the appraised value on the balance sheet as the amount of the asset.

_____ 6. JoAnn insists on including the full text of all 20 loan agreements in the financial statements for her company.

_____ 7. Fred has not generated financial statements for his company for five years and feels no need to determine profit or loss until the business is closed.

_____ 8. Frieda insists that her published financial statements balance to the penny and that all figures on the statements include dollars and cents to give financial statement users full information.

_____ 9. Joe received $250 today from a customer who wants products delivered next month. He recorded the collection as revenue.

_____ 10. Harry wants to present financial information as though he will not be in business past the end of the year.

_____ 11. Rosie wants to simply show the number of inventory items she has on hand rather than try to determine a dollar amount for them.

_____ 12. Because income was too high for the year, Don subtracted the entire amount the company paid for its new car.

A.	Separate entity assumption	G.	Matching principle
B.	Going-concern assumption	H.	Full disclosure principle
C.	Monetary unit assumption	I.	Materiality constraint
D.	Periodicity assumption	J.	Cost-benefit constraint
E.	Historical cost principle	K.	Conservatism
F.	Revenue recognition principle	L.	Industry practices

Basic Concepts of Accounting and Financial Reporting

2. Identify the statement(s) on which each of the following would appear.

___ 1. Cash	___ 11. Retained Earnings
___ 2. Revenues	___ 12. Accounts Payable
___ 3. Common Stock	___ 13. Net Income
___ 4. Gains	___ 14. Equipment
___ 5. Losses	___ 15. Net cash from operating
___ 6. Income tax expense	activities
___ 7. Accounts Receivable	___ 16. Dividends
___ 8. Gross Profit	___ 17. Wages expense
___ 9. Cost of goods sold	___ 18. Inventory
___ 10. Notes Payable	

A. Income Statement   C. Balance Sheet
B. Statement of Owners' Equity   D. Statement of Cash Flows

Exercises:

1. Fill in the missing information in each of the following condensed income statements:

A.
Sales	$25,000
Cost of goods sold	14,000
Gross profit	?
Expenses	9,000
Net income	$ 2,000

B.
Sales	$200,000
Cost of Goods Sold	?
Gross profit	?
Expenses	105,000
Net loss	$ (5,000)

C.
Sales	?
Cost of goods sold	92,000
Gross profit	$142,000
Expenses	?
Net income	$ 22,000

D.
Sales	$ 73,000
Cost of goods sold	75,000
Gross profit	$?
Expenses	5,000
Net loss	$ (7,000)

2. Complete the missing amounts in each of the following condensed statements of stockholders' equity:

A.
	Common Stock	Retained Earnings	Total
Beg. Bal.	$5,000	$3,000	$8,000
	-0-	7,300	7,300
End. Bal	$?	$?	$15,300

28

B.

	Common Stock	Retained Earnings	Total
Beg. Bal.	$10,000	$?	$17,000
	$25.000	6,300	31,300
End. Bal	?	$13,300	$48,300

3. Complete the missing values in the following condensed balance sheets:

A. Total assets $105,732   B. Total assets $?
    Total liabilities   73,205   Total liabilities   98,403
    Total equity   ?   Total equity   37,610

Problems:

1. The information below relates to the Owens Company as of December 31, 2004. Using the example statements in the text as your guide, prepare an income statement for the company (Hint: not all of the information will be needed). Remember to include the proper heading for your statement.

Sales	$300,000
Cost of goods sold	220,000
Cash	15,000
Equipment	45,000
Wage expense	3,000
Retained earnings (beginning of the year)	28,000
Notes payable	50,000
Land	30,000
Income tax expense	1,000
Selling expense	15,000
Common stock	15,000
Accounts payable	10,000
Inventory	60,000
Rent expense	4,000
Dividends	10,000

2. Now, using the information relating to the Owens Company, prepare a statement of stockholders' equity.

3.   Use the relevant information in Exercise 1 and the example statements in the text to prepare a balance sheet for the company. Remember to include the proper heading for your statement

4.   Indicate the areas of the preceding statements which articulate.

SOLUTIONS

Multiple Choice:

1.	D		10.	C
2.	B		11.	B
3.	C		12.	A
4.	A		13.	A
5.	C		14.	D
6.	C		15.	C
7.	D		16.	C
8.	C		17.	A
9.	A			

True / False:

1.   True
2.   True
3.   False; timeliness requires that the information be available in time to be used to *make* decisions.
4.   False; accounting information would be considered verifiable if several individuals working *independently* would agree on conclusions about the data.
5.   False; accounting information should be neutral or absent of bias that would influence reported information.
6.   False; consistency refers to the need for the same entity to conform to similar accounting policies and procedures from period to period.
7.   True
8.   True
9.   True
10.   False; equity may also be earned by the company through profitable operations.
11.   True
12.   False; expenses are actual sacrifices of assets as opposed to an obligation to sacrifice an asset.
13.   True
14.   True
15.   False; advertising costs and salespeople's wages are selling expenses, not the cost of the product being sold.

16. True
17. False; the most common presentation of comprehensive income is on the statement of stockholders' equity.
18. False; retained earnings does not represent cash; it only represents past net income of the company that has been kept in the company.
19. True
20. False; deducting the owner's daughter's college tuition is a violation of the separate entity assumption.

Matching:

1. 1. A
   2. L
   3. H
   4. K
   5. E
   6. J
   7. D
   8. I
   9. F
   10. B
   11. C
   12. G

2. 1. C
   2. A
   3. B, C
   4. A.
   5. A
   6. A
   7. C
   8. A
   9. A
   10. C
   11. B, C
   12. C
   13. A, B, D
   14. C
   15. D
   16. B, D
   17. A
   18. A, C

Exercises:

1. A. Gross profit, $11,000
   B. Cost of goods sold, $100,000; Gross profit, $100,000
   C. Sales, $234,000; Expenses, $120,000
   D. Gross profit, $(2,000)

2. A. Common Stock ending balance, $5,000
      Retained Earnings, ending balance, $10,300

   B. Retained Earnings, beginning balance, $7,000
      Common Stock, ending balance, $35,000

3. 1. Total equity, $32,527
   2. Total assets, $136,013

Problems:

1.

Owens Company
Income Statement
For the year ended December 31, 2004

Sales		$300,000
Cost of Goods Sold		220,000
Gross Profit		$ 80,000
Operating Expenses		
Wage Expenses	$ 3,000	
Selling Expenses	15,000	
Rent Expenses	4,000	
Total Operating Expenses		$ 22,000
Income before Taxes		58,000
Income Taxes		1,000
Net Income		$ 57,000

2.

Owens Company
Statement of Stockholders' Equity
For the year ended December 31, 2004

	Common Stock	Retained Earnings	Totals
Beginning Balances	$15,000	$28,000	$43,000
Net Income		57,000	57,000
Dividends		(10,000)	(10,000)
Ending Balances	$15,000	$75,000	$90,000

3.

Owens Company
Balance Sheet
December 31, 2004

Assets:

Cash	$15,000	
Inventory	60,000	
Land	30,000	
Equipment	45,000	
Total Assets		$150,000

Liabilities and Equity:
Liabilities:

Accounts Payable	$10,000	
Notes Payable	50,000	
Total Liabilities		$ 60,000
Equity:		
Common Stock	$15.000	
Retained Earnings	75,000	
Total Equity		90,000
Total Liabilities and Equity		$150,000

4.   (1)   From the income statement, the net income flows through to the statement of stockholders' equity to update the retained earnings account.

           (2)   From the statement of stockholders' equity, the common stock account and the retained earnings account flow through to the balance sheet.

Chapter 3
Organizing a Business:
Equity and Debt Financing

CHAPTER SUMMARY

LO 1: Identify the steps in organizing a business.

Starting a business encompasses far more work and preparation than many believe. The International Accounting Associates LLP sets forth seven items to consider before beginning operations. Organizers of businesses should first **(1) find competent people to be responsible for the four functions of the firm.** These four functions include operating, investing, financing, and decision-making. The second item to consider is the **(2) organizational form for the business.** Next, the organizers should **(3) research the industry and the product** and **(4) prepare a strategic plan.** With these initial steps accomplished, the organizers are ready to **(5) design internal controls for operations and information, (6) secure financing,** and **(7) prepare initial capital and operating budgets.**

LO 2: Describe a corporate organization structure and define the equity structure of a corporation.

The choice of competent people depends on specific criteria of the job and the organizers. Once that decision is made, however, the organizational form quickly becomes the primary consideration. The limited liability provision of the corporate form makes it very attractive to many business organizers. These organizers, called incorporators, must submit a **formal application, the articles of incorporation,** to create a corporation. The articles of incorporation **contain information about the corporation, its purpose, names of the incorporators, and details about the corporate stock.** Approval of the articles of incorporation by the state agency results in the **issuance of the corporate charter, the document which creates the legal entity.**

Three groups of people play dramatic roles in the success of the corporation. First, the **stockholders** provide cash to the corporation in return for shares of the company. **Stock certificates** provide the evidence of the stockholders' ownership. The stockholders are represented in company operations by the **board of directors,** a group of stockholders selected by their peers to shoulder the ultimate responsibility for managing the corporation. Management of the daily operations of the company accrues to the corporate officers, the chief executive officer (CEO), the chief financial officer (CFO), and the chief operating officer (COO). Very small corporations may not utilize all of these titles in their operations.

The charter specifies the number of shares the corporation is allowed to issue. These **authorized shares** may be increased during the life of the corporation by the corporate officers' request to the state agency. **Issued shares** are those which the company has sold, while **outstanding shares** are the number of shares still in the hands of the investors. If a difference exists between issued and outstanding shares, the difference is called **treasury stock;** treasury stock remains issued but is no longer outstanding. Corporations use two primary types of stock.

| LO 3: Compare and contrast the characteristics of common stock and preferred stock. |

The type of stock issued most by corporations is **common stock.** These stockholders own any part of the corporation that might be left, in case of liquidation, after payment of liabilities and preferred stockholders. This stock may have a par value which was set at the time of incorporation or may be no-par stock. Par value was once used to define legal capital, but this definition has been eliminated. Still, the idea of attaching a par value to stock continues even today. No-par stock, as might be inferred, has no par value attached to it.

Preferred stock, on the other hand, has some very specific characteristics attached to it. Preferred stock usually has a par value attached to it; this par value becomes important in case of dividend declaration since dividends are usually based on a percentage of par value. Also, preferred stockholders get dividends before the common stockholders can get any, and, in case of liquidation, preferred stockholders will get their money before the common stockholders will. Alternatively, the common stockholders will be more likely to see fluctuations in the value of stock.

When either class of stock sells for more than par value, the cash received must be shown in a particular way. The stock account records the number of shares sold at their par value. Additional amounts received by the corporation go into the additional paid-in capital account.

| LO 4: Research an industry for its particular characteristics and identify its major competitors |

Specialized knowledge is required to research the industry to learn the environment in which the company will operate. Several sources of information are easily accessible. **Trade organizations** collect and make available specialized information about the industry itself. These organizations may be found through internet searches or asking someone in the industry. The best part of these organizations is that they really want to help you because the industry will expand.

Other alternatives include **market research firms, industry guides, and business periodicals.** The problems inherent in these sources are that research firms are usually for-profit enterprises and will want to charge you, industry guides require that you pursue the research yourself without assistance, and business periodicals are for general business, not just the segment you want to research.

| LO 5: Prepare a strategic plan for a business. |

After the industry is more fully understood, the business will need to prepare a strategic plan to provide a road map for its operations. This plan guides senior management in making decisions for the company in fulfilling its mission and goals. A strategic plan starts with (1) developing the **company's mission and vision**. Next, (2) measurable goals and objectives must be set to identify the manner in which the organization will achieve its goals. (3) The scan of the **internal environment** identifies the organization's culture and resources to assess strengths and weaknesses. Core competencies can be identified. The examination of the **external environment** allows analysis of the company's opportunities and threats. Having gone through these analyses, the company is now able to (4) **formulate alternative strategies** that will enable it to accomplish its goals. (5) Selection of the best of these alternatives provides the company with the ability to **develop the plan** to be accomplish goals. At this point, then, the organization can (6) **implement the plan** and then (7) **evaluate the results** which provide feedback to improve future plans.

> **LO 6: Outline internal controls for operations.**

In addition to having a strong strategic focus, the company must also implement and maintain a strong system of internal controls. These controls help protect against losses and promote efficiency in the accounting and operating processes. The most important of these controls require that the organization (1) **protect physical assets**, (2) **protect proprietary information**, and (3) **create the right environment** through management's tone in communicating the need for such measures.

Now that the company has a strategic plan to direct its activities and internal controls to provide protection for assets, the company must turn to financing of the business. Financing can be accomplished in two primary ways: internal or external. For start-up companies, the financing must first come from external sources.

> **LO 7: Define borrowing terms and compute the cost of borrowing.**

External financing may be from sale of shares of the business, a method which is generally called equity financing. The other alternative is by utilizing debt financing through borrowing, generally from financial institutions. Borrowing may be either **short-term**, requiring repayment in five years or less, or **long-term**, for longer than five years, depending on the needs of the company and its general credit rating. In either case, debt financing requires repayment at a specific point in time and the payment of interest at intervals of one year or less. The interest calculation is the one you learned in school: $I = PRT$. The borrowed amount times the annual interest rate times that portion of a year for which the loan has been outstanding will yield the amount of interest due. Interest is an expense for the borrower. Interest accrues from the day following the loan through the day of payment.

If the company enters into an agreement to borrow money, the lender may require that the agreement be a written promissory note such as a note payable. A longer term borrowing such as that needed to purchase buildings is a mortgage payable. Mortgages and some notes require that some asset be identified to be forfeited by the borrower in case of default. The asset constitutes collateral for the loan.

> **LO 8: Compute and distinguish between nominal and effective interest rates.**

On occasion, a lender may write a not which specifies a rate of interest on the full loan amount but then takes the interest amount out of the proceeds. The effect of this action means that the borrower is paying interest on the borrowed amount but has a lower amount of funds to use. **The effective interest rate is higher than the specified rate** because the borrower has used less money. To determine the true (effective) interest rate, the borrower would need to **divide the interest paid by the actual amount of funds available for use.** A note structured in this manner is called a discounted note. The interest rate specified on the note, **the nominal rate**, is not the true rate being charged.

This idea of adjusting the interest rate by proving less money to be used by the borrower can help in understanding the bonds that many large corporations use to borrow large sums of money. When the short-term **commercial paper**, a corporate promissory note, does not provide the corporation with funds needed, a larger financial market may be required. The bond market serves this purpose. Bonds are issued by corporations as a means of borrowing large sums of money for extended periods of time. The corporation issues a **bond indenture** which specifies the interest rate to be paid, the timing of the interest payments, and the due date of the bond. **Par value** of the bond is the stated amount the corporation wishes to borrow. Since the interest rate is specified with regard to the principal of the loan, buyers of the bonds know exactly how much cash they will receive in interest. They can, however, adjust the effective interest by adjusting the amount they lend to the corporation.

The selling price of the bond may be higher, lower, or equal to par value. If, the buyers of the bonds want a higher **effective interest rate,** they would lend less money to the corporation; the bonds would sell at a **discount**. If the buyers require a lower effective interest rate, they would bid higher on the bonds, and the bonds would sell at a **premium**. A price exactly equal to par value leads to the effective interest rate being exactly equal to the nominal rate.

The corporation itself is only concerned with the price received for bonds on the date they are first sold. Only at the initial sale does the money go to the issuing corporation. This particular sale of bonds occurs in the **primary securities market.** Later, people who bought the bonds can sell them and others can buy the bonds in the **secondary securities market**. These trades are among investors only, and the issuing corporation receives nothing from the trades.

LO 9: Compute the selling price of bonds with a calculator.

Financial calculators allow the computation of effective interest rate, or yield, and the selling price of a bond.

Although differences exist among models, most operate in a similar manner. To find the selling price of a bond, you must enter the following:

n = the number of interest payment periods
i = the effective interest rate per period
FV = maturity value (face value of the bond)
P = cash interest paid each period
cpt = tells the calculator to compute
PV = selling price of the bonds.

This calculation permits buyers of bonds to determine the price to be paid in order to accrue the required return on their investment.

CHAPTER GLOSSARY

Additional paid-in capital: the amount paid to a corporation for stock in excess of its par value

Articles of incorporation: an application for incorporation that generally includes: (1) basic information about the corporation and its purpose; (2) the names of the incorporators; and (3) details concerning the types and amounts of corporate stock authorized for sale

Authorized shares: the maximum number of shares the charter allows the corporation to issue

Bond: a type of long-term note payable, usually a $1,000 interest-bearing debt instrument

Bond indenture: a legal document that details the agreement between the company issuing the bonds and the buyers of the bonds, including the timing and amount of the interest payments and repayment of the bond principal

Chief operating officer (COO): the corporate officer who directs the daily operations of the corporation

Collateral: something of value that must be forfeited to the lender if the borrower fails to make payments as agreed

Commercial paper: a corporate promissory note that investors buy from the corporation

Common stock: the voting stock of a corporation

Core competency: an activity at the center of the organization's purpose that it performs very well

Corporate bylaws: basic rules for management to follow in conducting the corporation's business

Corporate charter: a certificate that creates a legal corporate entity and entitles the corporation to begin operations

Corporate mission: a statement that describes the organization's purpose

Organizing a Business: Debt and Equity Financing

Corporate secretary: the corporate officer who maintains the minutes of the board of directors' and stockholders' meetings and may also represent the company in legal proceedings

Corporate stock: evidence of a share of ownership in a corporation

Corporate vision: a statement that articulates the organization's values and intentions

Debt financing: borrowing funds for business operations

Default: failure to repay a loan as agreed or to abide by other requirements of the lending agreement

Discount: occurs when a bond sells for less than par value

Discounted note: a loan arrangement in which a bank deducts the full interest in advance from the loan proceeds

Effective interest rate: the actual interest rate the lender earns and the borrower pays

Effective interest rate of a bond: the actual interest rate that the bondholder will earn over the life of the bond; also called the **yield rate** or **market interest rate**

Equity financing: acquiring funds for business operations by selling ownership interests in the company

External environment: the industry environment and the macroenvironment in which a company operates

Incorporators: persons who submit a formal application to create a corporation and file it with the appropriate state agency

Industry: a group of companies that form a sector of the economy

Industry environment: a company's relationships and relative power position with its customers, suppliers, competitors, special interest groups, and the extent of substitute products and services

Interest: the cost of borrowing money and represents rent paid to use another's money. It is revenue to the lender and expense to the borrower

Internal environment: an organization's culture and resources

Issued shares: shares of stock sold to stockholders

Liquidation: the process of going out of business when all assets are sold and all liabilities are settled

Long-term financing: borrowing with a repayment period that extends past five years

Macroenvironment: the current and future state of, and likely changes in, the economic climate, the political climate, demographics, technology, and societal trends and attitudes

Mortgage: a document that states the agreement between a lender and a borrower who has secured the loan with collateral

Nominal interest rate: the interest rate that the issuing corporation agreed to pay in the bond indenture, stated as a percentage of the par value of the bond

No-par stock: stock authorized without a par value

Note payable: a written agreement or debt instrument between a lender and a borrower that creates a liability for the borrower to repay both principal and interest

Outstanding shares: the number of shares of stock currently held by stockholders

Par value: an arbitrary dollar amount placed on the stock by the incorporators at the time of incorporation

Par value stock: stock that carries a par value

Par value for a bond: the principal of the loan, which is the amount that must be repaid at maturity

Preferred stock: stock that offers certain preferential treatment to its owners over common stockholders for dividends and in the event of liquidation

Premium: occurs when a bond sells for more than par value

Primary securities market: sales of newly issued stocks and bonds between the issuing corporation and investors where the corporation receives the proceeds of sales

Principal: in the case of notes and mortgages, the amount of funds actually borrowed

Promissory note: a legal promise to repay a loan

Secondary securities market: trading that occurs on organized stock exchanges among buying and selling investors, and the corporation receives nothing from these trades

Selling price of a bond: the amount for which a bond actually sells. Also called the **market price**

Short-term financing: borrowing that must be repaid within five years

Stock certificate: a legal document providing evidence of ownership and containing the provisions of the stock ownership agreement

Strategic plan: the plan that describes the organizational approach the senior management of a company will employ to fulfill the corporate mission and vision and achieve the stated goals by allocating financial resources and directing human resources

Term: the length of time between borrowing and repaying the loan

Trade organizations: organizations that collect information about the industry, act as a spokesperson for the industry, interface with government agencies, and promote the products and services marketed by the industry

Treasurer: the corporate officer who is responsible for managing the company's cash

Treasury stock: shares of stock reacquired by the corporation and held in the treasury

PROBLEM APPLICATIONS

Multiple Choice Questions:

For each of the following multiple choice questions, circle the letter of the BEST response.

1. Which of the following classifications of shares would be represented by the largest number of shares?
   A. Issued shares
   B. Treasury shares
   C. Authorized shares
   D. Outstanding shares

2. A stock certificate
   A. is a legal document providing evidence of ownership.
   B. contains general information about the corporation and its purpose
   C. is a certificate that creates a legal corporate entity
   D. contains the corporate bylaws which serve as basic rules for management to follow in conducting the corporation's business.

3. Which of the following groups or individuals is elected by the stockholders?
   A. Board of directors
   B. Chief Executive Officer
   C. Treasurer
   D. Corporate Secretary

4. Par value for common stock is
   A. The amount for which the stock is sold.
   B. An arbitrary dollar amount placed on stock by incorporators at the time of sale.
   C. An arbitrary dollar amount placed on stock by incorporators at the time of incorporation.
   D. The amount that the stock can be exchanged for in the event of liquidation.

5. The four functions of the firm include
   A. operating, investing, managing, and financing.
   B. operating, investing, managing, and organizing.
   C. operating, investing, financing, and decision-making.
   D. investing, financing, managing, and organizing.

6. The individuals ultimately responsible for managing the affairs of the corporation are
   A. the CEO, the CFO, and the COO.
   B. the board of directors.
   C. the stockholders.
   D. the incorporators.

7. The quarterly dividend for a share of $100 par value 10% preferred stock would be
   A. $10.00.
   B. $5.00.
   C. $2.50.
   D. impossible to determine.

8. The most direct and economical means of researching an industry is through
   A. market research firms.
   B. business periodicals.
   C. on-line databases.
   D. trade organizations.

9. The internal environment of a company includes
   A. beliefs, values, and expectations of personnel.
   B. maintenance agreements.
   C. the company's macroenvironment.
   D. the number of competitors the company has.

10. If you borrowed $25,000 for four months at an 8 percent interest rate, how much would you have to repay when the loan is due (rounded to the nearest whole dollar)?
   A. 667
   B. 2,000
   C. 25,000
   D. 25,667

True / False Questions:

1. Preferred stock is called preferred because it has preferential treatment over common shareholders for dividends and in the event of liquidation.
2. Internal control measures would include giving access to assets as well as record keeping duties related to those assets to one trusted employee.
3. Small businesses have two primary sources of financing – owners and banks or other financing institutions.
4. Interest on borrowed funds is considered a revenue to the lender and an expense to the borrower.
5. Corporate bylaws generally include basic information about the corporation as well as details concerning the types and amount of corporate stock for sale.
6. The number of treasury shares plus the number of issued shares equal the number of outstanding shares.
7. Par value for common stock is an arbitrary dollar amount placed on stock by incorporators at the time of incorporation.
8. Equity financing acquires funds by selling ownership interests in the company whereas debt financing acquires funds by borrowing for business operations.
9. A discounted note is a loan agreement in which a bank offers a discounted interest rate to the borrower.
10. A secondary securities market is where trading occurs on organized stock exchanges among buying and selling investors and the corporation receives nothing from these trades.

Matching: Match each of the following items with their definitions.

_____	1.	Collateral	_____	7.	Default
_____	2.	Discount	_____	8.	Effective interest rate
_____	3.	Term	_____	9.	Nominal interest rate
_____	4.	Stated rate	_____	10.	Promissory note
_____	5.	Discounted note	_____	11.	Bond indenture
_____	6.	Premium			

A. The actual interest rate paid by the borrower.
B. Result when bonds sell for less than par value.
C. A legal promise to repay a loan.
D. A loan arrangement in which a bank deducts the full interest in advance from the loan proceeds.
E. The interest rate that the issuing corporation agreed to pay, stated as a percentage of the par value of a bond.
F   Result when bonds sell for more than par value.
G. Something of value that must be forfeited to the lender if the borrower fails to make payments as agreed.
H. The length of time to maturity of the loan.
I. Failure of a borrower to meet the terms of the loan agreement.
J. An agreement that sets forth the terms of a bond.

Problems:

1. Short-a-Cash Company borrowed $20,000 on November 1, 2003 from First Bank by signing a note payable at 8% interest due in one year. The terms of the note required that repayment of principal and interest was to be made one year from the date of the note.

    REQUIRED:

    a. What is the revenue First Bank will record for this loan in 2003?

    b. How much will Short-a-Cash Company have to repay when the note is due?

2.   The equity section of Our Company follows:

Preferred Stock, 9,750 shares issued	$975,000
Common Stock, 100,000 shares authorized,	
25,000 shares issued	250,000
Additional paid-in capital, common stock	75,000
Treasury stock, 5,000 shares	(60,000)

REQUIRED:

a.   Determine par value for the preferred stock.

b.   What is par value for the common stock?

c.   On average, for what price did the common stock sell?

d.   How many shares of common are outstanding?

e.   If the preferred stock paid dividends of 10% annually, how much would be paid to preferred stockholders in dividends each year?

3.   Using a financial calculator, compute the amount to be paid for each of the following bond issues (be sure to write down the variables you use):

a. $500,000 of bonds with a stated interest rate of 7%, due to mature in 10 years. Interest is paid each year, and the buyers of the bonds want an 8% return on their investment.

b. $700,000 of bonds with a stated interest rate of 10%, due to mature in 5 years. Interest is paid each year, and the buyers of the bonds want to get a 9% return on their investment.

4.   If a company sells $750,000 of bonds, which pay 10% interest each year and mature in 5 years, for $783,000, what is the total amount the company would have to pay to borrow the money (the total cost of the borrowing)?

5.   If a company sells $200,000 of bonds which pay 7% interest each year for 5 years at a price of $195,000, what is the total cost of the borrowing?

SOLUTIONS

Multiple Choice:

1.	C		6.	B
2.	A		7.	C
3.	A		8.	D
4.	C		9.	A
5.	C		10.	D

True / False:

1. True
2. False; duties should be segregated such that each employee has controlled access to assets and no employee with access to assets should have access to alter record keeping for that asset.
3. True
4. True
5. False; corporate bylaws are the basic rules for management to follow in conducting the corporation's business.
6. False; the number of issued shares minus the number of treasury shares equals the number of outstanding shares which could be rewritten as the number of treasury shares plus the number of outstanding shares equals the number of issued shares.
7. True
8. True
9. False; a discounted note is a loan arrangement in which a bank deducts the full interest in advance from the loan proceeds.
10. True

Matching:

1.	G		7.	I
2.	B		8.	A
3.	H		9.	E
4.	E		10.	C
5.	D		11.	J
6.	F			

Problems:

1.   (a) $20,000 times 8% interest times 2/12 = $266.67
       (b)   Interest of $1,600 + Principal of $20,000 = $21,600.

2.   (a) $975,000 ÷ 9,750 shares = $100 per share
       (b) $250,000 ÷ 25,000 = $10 per share
       (c)   ($250,000 + $75,000) ÷ 25,000 shares = $13 per share
       (d)   25,000 shares − 5,000 shares = 20,000 outstanding
       (e) $975,000 times 10% = $97,500 per year

3.   (a) $n = 10$
             $i = 8\%$
             FV = $500,000
             P = $500,000 times 7% = $35,000 per year
             PV = $466.450 (approximately)

       (b) $n = 5$
             $i = 9\%$
             FV = $700,000
             P = $700,000 times 10% = $70,000 per year
             PV = $727,228 (approximately)

4. $ 750,000 times 10% times 5 years = $375,000 (total interest to be paid)
                                      750,000 (principal paid)
                            $1,125,000 (total payments)
                     Less   783,000 (amount received for bonds)
                          $ 342,000   net cost of borrowing

5. $200,000 times 7% times 5 years = $ 70,000 (total interest to be paid)
                                  200,000 (principal paid)
                          $270,000 (total payments)
                    Less   195,000 (amount received for bonds)
                       $ 75,000 net cost of borrowing

Chapter 4
Planning for and
Predicting Performance

CHAPTER SUMMARY

One of the first activities that must be accomplished in starting any business is to get a good idea of the costs that will be incurred. Costs of buying equipment, financing, operating, and all of the other activities must be considered as well as the method of generating the funds to cover these costs. Without a plan for the amounts to be spent and the method of paying the costs, any business has a distinct disadvantage. To avoid this disadvantage, businesses must start with a budgeting process as an analytical tool. Developing a budget quickly leads to the realization that an understanding of the nature of cost behavior is required to be able to budget effectively.

> **LO 1: Classify costs by cost objects and cost drivers and describe the characteristics of activity-based cost systems and standard cost systems.**

The classifications of costs will probably depend on the decision to be made by using them. One often-used classification criterion is by **cost object.** A cost object is an area of the business for which management has incurred a cost and wants it separately measured. These may be products, regions, projects, or other aspects of the business for which the measurement of costs is desired.

Some costs occur specifically for a given cost object; these costs are called **direct costs.** Other costs are shared by various cost objects and are, therefore, labeled **common costs.** In order to know the full cost of the cost object, both direct and common costs must be included.

Two systems have been developed to aid companies in their cost management. The newest of these is the **activity-based costing (ABC) system.** In this system, managers identify activities, called **cost drivers,** that cause costs to be incurred. The purpose of ABC systems relates to their improved allocation abilities since the costs are closely aligned with the driver.

Standard cost systems have served companies well in providing benchmarks of performance. With a benchmark, management knows the cost of given activities and products that should be incurred. Actual costs can then be compared with these standard costs to determine whether cost management is improving, deteriorating, or maintaining. If the costs are deemed to be out of line, managers can focus on problem areas and resolve problems early.

Planning for and Predicting Performance

LO 2: Distinguish between product and period costs.

In order to provide financial accounting information to people outside the organization, costs must be separated in another manner. Since products can be inventoried, **product costs** must be identified and kept separate from **period costs.** Product costs provide the amounts that attach to units of product and are later released as cost of goods sold. Period costs are generally expensed as they are incurred.

Period costs include **selling costs**, the costs of getting the product into the hands of the buyer, and **administrative costs**, the other costs incurred in operating a business. Selling costs encompass items like advertising, salespeople's salaries and commissions, shipping product to the customer, etc. Administrative costs describe activities like the cost of the accounting department, the president's salary, etc. Though peripheral to the main purpose of the company, these administrative functions are necessary to maintain the environment for the business to operate.

LO 3: Differentiate between fixed and variable costs and classify costs by cost behavior.

Another method of segregating costs relates to the behavior of the costs. Some depend on the degree of activity in the business while others are a given amount regardless of how busy (or idle) the company may be. **Fixed costs** occur as large amounts without regard to whether the company is busy or idle. Rent on a building, for example, will cost the same amount each month whether the business is making money or not. The nice part about fixed costs is that when the business starts to do well, the cost will still be the same amount. **Variable costs** change with activity levels. If, for instance, the company makes 500 units of product, material costs will be 500 times the cost of one unit of product. If no units of product are produced, material costs will go to zero. A **mixed cost** is what it says—mixed. It contains some fixed cost and some variable cost.

LO 4: Explain the concept of a relevant range and its effect on cost information.

Company personnel can use the ideas of fixed and variable costs to predict costs to be incurred in the future with specified levels of activity. An important restriction on these predictions, however, lies in the fact that the predictions can only be valid within the **relevant range**. This range defines the area in which we can anticipate that the cost analyses will hold true. Outside the relevant range, cost behavior can change enough that all predictions are invalid. Because company personnel are depending on the numbers derived in predictions about cost, they must know the area in which the numbers provided will give them good information. Whether a cost is variable, fixed, or mixed, the assumptions about its behavior only hold true within the relevant range.

LO 5: Analyze cost information to construct a total cost formula for a business activity.

To the extent company personnel can identify the relevant range and make predictions within it, they can utilize the total cost formula to predict the cost to be incurred at a given level of production. The formula requires identification of the fixed costs in total, the variable costs per unit of product, and an estimate of the total amount of production anticipated. The formula simply states that the fixed costs in total plus the total variable costs (the product of the variable costs per unit times the number of units) equals the total costs.

Knowledge of cost behavior also allows the construction of a new kind of financial statement, one based on cost behavior rather than product and period costs. The income statement presented earlier in the text was based on the segregation of costs according to purpose, either product or period, in determining operating income. These same costs can be divided by cost behavior and used to construct a **contribution margin income statement.** This statement first subtracts variable expenses from revenue to get the contribution margin; then the fixed expenses are subtracted to get the operating income. The operating income is the same as that found in the previous income statement. Now, however, the user of the statement knows more about cost behavior and how much of the revenues are "contributed" toward coverage of fixed expenses. This form of statement also proves useful in analysis of the relationships between costs and volume.

LO 6: Conduct cost-volume-profit analysis to determine break-even points.

Cost-volume-profit (CVP) analysis utilizes the information that has been gathered about cost behavior to let management determine the effects of changes in price, volume, variable costs or fixed costs. A basic calculation of CVP analysis is the computation of **breakeven**, that point at which all costs are covered, but no profit occurs. The formula utilized is the formula for the contribution margin income statement: sales - variable costs = contribution margin and contribution margin - fixed costs = operating income. At the point of equality between contribution margin and fixed costs, operating income would equal zero, and the company would break even.

An additional tool that can be derived from the CVP analysis is the **contribution margin ratio (CMR).** The ratio is found by dividing contribution margin in dollars by sales in dollars. The resulting percentage identifies that portion of each sales dollar that goes to coverage of fixed costs. Dividing fixed costs by the contribution margin ratio yields the dollar amount of sales required to achieve breakeven.

LO 7: Perform sensitivity analysis.

The dynamic nature of business dictates that change always occurs. CVP analysis provides a tool to estimate the effect of changes on net income. This analysis of changes in the CVP relationships is called **sensitivity analysis.** It lets managers get insights into the potential effects of what-if questions such as price changes or changes in variable or fixed costs. Potential changes can be entered into the formula to predict the outcomes of possible changes.

LO 8: Build initial operating and capital budgets.

With these tools in mind, new business managers can start to build initial budgets (or existing managers can budget with much more knowledge). The **operating budget** requires estimates of the types of on-going expenses the company will incur over a given period of time. A monthly budget is preferable. Almost all information will need to be estimated; the need to estimate does not mean that guesses are acceptable. More accuracy in the budget will yield much better information for the managers. A great deal of research into historical data and others' experiences will be required of the first-time budget maker. Dividing the costs by function and by cost behavior will aid in later analyses also.

Additionally, a budget for **capital items** must also be developed. The items are generally one-time expenses or, at the least, expenses that will not be incurred in a short time. These items include purchases of machinery, furnishings, intangibles, and computers, for example, as well as start-up costs such as costs of incorporation and start-up expenditures. Sources and uses of cash should be identified. Finally, performing break-even analysis gives the entrepreneurs a perspective on the number of products that must be sold for the company to achieve breakeven.

CHAPTER GLOSSARY

Activity-based costing (ABC) system: a cost system that identifies specific activities that cause costs to occur and uses these activities as the bases for common cost allocation

Administrative costs: all costs of operating a business that are not product and selling costs. Includes support functions such as accounting, finance, executive, and human resources

Amortization: allocation of costs of intangible assets to the time periods benefited

Breakeven: occurs when a company's operating income is zero

Break-even point: the sales volume required to achieve breakeven

Capital budget: A budget that outlines how a company intends to allocate its scarce resources to purchase major investments in long-lived assets for current and future years

Common costs: costs shared by a number of cost objects

Contribution income statement: an income statement that classifies expenses by cost behavior

Contribution margin: the difference between operating revenues and variable costs, which measures the amount of revenues remaining after variable costs to contribute toward fixed costs and profits

Contribution margin ratio: the contribution margin divided by sales

Cost driver: the activity that causes an expense to occur

Cost object: an activity, product, service, project, geographic region, or business segment for which management wants separate cost measurement

Cost-volume-profit (CVP) analysis: the analysis of the relationships between cost and volume, and the effect of those relationships on profit

Direct costs: costs easily traced to one cost object

Fixed cost: a cost that remains the same regardless of the volume of sales or production

Intangible assets: assets consisting of contractual rights

Mixed cost: a cost that has both a fixed component and a variable component

Operating budget: a budget that plans a company's routine business activities for one to five years

Period costs: the costs of operating a business that are not product costs

Product costs: all costs of acquiring or manufacturing goods to make them available for sale to customers

Relevant range: a range of business activity in which cost-behavior patterns remain unchanged

Selling costs: period costs related to advertising, selling, and delivering goods to customers

Sensitivity analysis: a technique used to determine the effect of changes on the CVP relationship

Standard: a preestablished benchmark for desirable performance

Standard cost system: a system in which management sets cost standards and uses them to evaluate actual performance

Variable cost: a cost that changes proportionately with the volume of sales or production

PROBLEM APPLICATIONS

Multiple Choice Questions:

For each of the following multiple choice questions, circle the letter of the BEST answer.

1. A capital budget
   A. outlines how a company intends to allocate its scare resources to purchase major investments in long-lived assets for current and future years.
   B. classifies expenses by cost behavior.
   C. analyzes the relationships between cost and volume, and the effect of those relationships on profit.
   D. plans a company's future business activities for one to five years.

2. A standard cost system
   A. provides the industry norm for performance.
   B. establishes benchmarks against which current performance is evaluated.
   C. is used by the largest firms in an industry.
   D. sets a base line for minimum performance.

3. The construction of a contribution margin income statement
   A. requires elimination of mixed costs from the system.
   B. requires separation of mixed costs into variable and fixed costs.
   C. requires a degree in cost analysis.
   D. yields a different income figure than does a statement based on product and period costs.

4. A relevant range is a range of business activity in which
   A. a company's profit remains unchanged.
   B. breakeven can be achieved.
   C. cost behavior patterns remain unchanged.
   D. standard costs apply.

5. Break-even in units can be described as fixed costs divided by
   A. contribution margin per unit
   B. contribution margin ratio
   C. sales price per unit
   D. variable cost per unit

6. A graph of a fixed cost, within the relevant range
   A. shows a horizontal line across production levels.
   B. shows a constantly increasing line across production levels.
   C. shows a horizontal line to a point and then a constantly increasing line.
   D. shows a line with no discernible pattern.

7. For common cost allocation, an activity-based costing system uses a cost
    A. planner
    B. driver
    C. goal
    D. standard

True / False Questions:

1. A capital budget plans a company's routine business activities for one to five years.
2. A cost object is an activity, product, service, project, geographic region, or business segment for which management desires separate cost measurement.
3. An activity-based costing system identifies the specific activity that causes a cost to occur and uses that activity as the basis for common cost allocation.
4. Product costs are all of the costs of operating a business.
5. Period costs include both selling and administrative costs.
6. Total variable costs do not change in total within the relevant range.
7. The total cost formula is total cost equals variable costs plus product costs.
8. Calculation of total cost requires knowledge of an estimated level of production.
9. Breakeven occurs when a company's operating income is zero.
10. Contribution margin ratio is the contribution margin divided by sales.

Matching: Match each numbered term with its lettered definition.

_____ 1 Capital budget	_____ 6 Cost driver
_____ 2 Variable cost	_____ 7 Mixed cost
_____ 3 Period costs	_____ 8 Operating budget
_____ 4 Common costs	_____ 9 Product costs
_____ 5 Direct costs	_____ 10 Fixed costs

A.   Costs easily traced to one cost object

B.   A budget that plans a company's routine business activities for one to five years

C.   All costs of acquiring or manufacturing goods to make them available for sale to customers

D.   A cost that has both a fixed and a variable component

E.   The activity that causes an expense to occur

F.   A budget that outlines how a company intends to allocate its scarce resources to purchase major investments in long-lived assets for current and future years

G.   The costs of operating a business that are not product costs

H.   A cost that changes proportionately, in total, with the volume of sales or production

I.   Costs shared by a number of cost objects

J.   A cost that remains the same regardless of the volume of sales or production

Exercises:

1. Steven's Company custom prints t-shirts for specific orders. The contribution margin income statement for Steven's Company for the last month is shown below:

Steven's Company
Contribution Income Statement
For the month ended May 31, 2005

		Totals	Unit
Sales		$21,000	$30.00
Less: Variable costs			
Cost of goods sold		10,500	15.00
Printing		2,100	3.00
Contribution margin		$ 8,400	$12.00
Less: Fixed costs			
Rent Expense	$ 950		
Salary Expense	3,000		
Insurance Expense	1,500		
Total Fixed Costs		5,450	
Operating Income		$ 2,950	

Required: Answer each of the following questions:

a. What is Steven's break even in units?
b. What is Steven's break even in dollars?
c. What is Steven's total cost formula?
d. How many units is Steven currently selling?
e. What is Steven's current operating income if the income statement is constructed using the product and period cost format?
e. What would net income be if Steven sold 50 more units next month?

2. Complete the blanks in each of the following independent cases:

Case	Units Sold	Sales	Variable Expenses	Contribution Margin per Unit	Fixed Expenses	Net Income (Loss)
A	1,500	$18,000	$12,000	$_____	$5,000	$_____
B	_____	100,000	_____	10	32,000	8,000
C	10,000	_____	70,000	13	_____	12,000
D	6,000	300,000	_____	_____	100,000	(10,000)

Problems:

1. Jones Manufacturing Company manufactures backpacks. The company currently is incurring the following costs during the month of May, 2005:

Materials:	$20 per backpack
Labor: (2 hours)	10 per backpack
Variable Mfg. Costs	2 per backpack
Fixed Mfg. Costs	$5,000 per month
Variable Selling Costs	3 per backpack
Fixed Selling Costs	$ 500 per month
Selling price	$60 per backpack

Required: Determine each of the following for Jones:

a. Construct the total cost formula for Jones.
b. If Jones can sell 1,000 backpacks, what will the totals costs be?
c. What would be the cost for manufacturing 1,250 backpacks?
d. Assume that Jones can sell all 1,250 backpacks. Construct a contribution margin income statement for the month of August, 2005.
e. Now, construct an income statement using product and period costs. How do the operating income figures compare between the two?
f. Using CVP analysis, determine Jones' break-even point in dollars and in units.
g. What would be the effect on Jones' net income if the company paid $500 for advertising which is predicted to raise the units sold to 1,300?

2. Construct an operating budget for Jones Manufacturing Company for next month assuming the company plans to sell 1,500 backpacks at $60 per backpack. All other costs specified in #1 above remain in effect. Additionally, the company has entered into an advertising program which costs $700 per month. The company pays taxes at a 30% rate on net income.

SOLUTIONS

Multiple Choice:

1.	A
2.	B
3.	B
4.	C
5.	A
6.	A
7.	B

True / False:

1. False; a capital budget outlines how a company intends to allocate its scare resources to purchase major investments in long-lived assets for current and future years.
2. True
3. True
4. False; product costs are all costs of acquiring or manufacturing goods to make them available for sale to customers and do no include non-product related operational cost.
5. True
6. False; variable costs per unit do not change within the relevant range, but total variable cost will change proportionately with the volume of sales or production.
7. False; total cost equals total variable costs plus fixed costs.
8. True
9. True
10. True

Matching:

1.	F
2.	H
3.	G
4.	I
5.	A
6.	E
7.	D
8.	B
9.	C
10.	J

Exercises:

1.
   a. $\$5450 \div \$12 = 455$ units (actually 454.167, but we can't make or sell partial units) to break even
   b. $\$5450 \div 40\% = \$13,625$ to break even
   c. $TC = \$5,450 + \$18X$ (where X = number of units manufactured)
   d. $\$21,000 \div \$30$ per unit = 700 units.
   e. Operating income using a different format would be the same, $\$2,950$.
   f. 50 units times $\$12$ per unit CM = $\$600 + \$2,950 = \$3,550$ next month

2. a. CM per unit = $4; net income = $1,000
    b. 4,000 units sold; variable expenses = $60,000.
    c. Sales = $200,000; fixed expenses = $118,000
    d. Variable expenses = $210,000; CM per unit = $15

Problems:

1. a. TC = $5,500 + $35 X
    b. $5,500 + $35 (1,000) = $40,500
    c. $5,500 + $35 (1,250) = $49,250
    d.

Jones Manufacturing Company
Contribution Income Statement
For the month ended May 31, 2005

		Total	Unit
Sales		$75,000	$60
Less: Variable expenses			
Materials	$25,000		20
Labor	12,500		10
Other manufacturing	2,500		2
Selling	3,750		3
Total Variable		43,750	
Contribution margin		$31,250	$25
Less: Fixed expenses			
Manufacturing	$ 5,000		
Selling	500		
Total Fixed		5,500	
Operating income		$25,750	

e.

Jones Manufacturing Company
Income Statement
For the month ended May 31, 2005

Sales	$75,000
Less: Cost of Goods Sold	45,000
Gross Margin	$30,000
Less: Selling Expenses	4,250
Operating Income	$25,750

No difference occurs in the operating income; only the format has changed.

f. $5,500 ÷ $25 = 220 backpacks

g. Contribution margin on 1,300 units   =   1,300 times $25 = $32,500
    - Fixed expenses ($5,500 from above + $500 Advertising   =   6,000
                    Predicted net income $26,500
                Less: current net income   25,750
        Increase in net income with advertising program $ 750

2.

Jones Manufacturing Company
Operating Budget
For the month ended June 30, 2005

Budgeted sales (1,500 units @ $60) $ 90,000
Budgeted variable expenses (1,500 units @ $35)   52,500
Budgeted contribution margin (1,500 units @ $25 $ 37,500
Budgeted fixed expenses ($5,500 + $700)   6,200
            Budgeted income before taxes $ 31,300
Less: Estimated income taxes (30%)   9,390

Chapter 5
Recording Accounting Data

CHAPTER SUMMARY

LO 1: Identify and describe the eight steps of the accounting cycle.

Through an understanding of the manner in which data are accumulated and combined, the financial statement user can develop a greater understanding of the statement information. The development of financial statements occurs through an eight-step process, beginning with **(1) an analysis of transactions**. The transactions to be included in a given set of financial statements must relate to the time period of the statements and at least two changes in the elements of the financial statements must have occurred. Once the decision has been made that a transaction has occurred in the current accounting period, the **(2) transaction must be journalized.** Journal entries provide a listing of the transactions, generally in the chronological order in which they occurred. The journal can be a special journal or a general journal. The third step allows for data about a given item to be summarized in one place. In this step, the **(3) journal entries are posted to the general ledger.** The items to which the posting is done are called **accounts**. A listing of all accounts, called the **chart of accounts**, is kept with their account numbers in order that people can find the information about specific items easily.

At the end of the accounting period, whether that time period is a month, a quarter, or a year, the remaining steps in the accounting cycle take place. The next step, after all journal entries have been posted, is to **(4) take a trial balance.** The trial balance does nothing but prove that the equality of the accounting equation has been maintained. Some companies use the worksheet format to determine this equality and to also complete the remaining steps in the accounting cycle. Next, the accountant needs to be sure of the correct measuring of revenues and expenses. This step requires **(5) adjusting the accounts and reconciling the bank account.** Sometimes revenues are earned or expenses are incurred, but no document has been made to show that fact. Revenues or expenses may **accrue** (be earned or used) without their being recognized. Likewise, items paid in advance, called **deferrals**, may have been earned or used during the period. Additionally, errors may have been found that require **error correction.**

Once the preceding steps have been taken, the accountant has some confidence that the account balances are correct so **(6) financial statements can be prepared.** The next step, then, is to prepare for the next accounting cycle by **(7) preparing and posting the closing entries.** Closing entries clear the balances from the accounts used to measure items for a given period of time and puts those balances into the accounts that are found on the balance sheet. All revenue accounts are closed to income summary, and all expense accounts are closed to income summary. The income summary and dividend accounts are then closed to retained earnings. Now, the only accounts which have balances are the accounts that are found on the balance sheet. To make sure the equality has been retained, then, the last step is to **(8) prepare a post-closing trial balance.** The post-closing trial balance assures the accountant of the equality of the accounting equation for the accounts with balances—all of those accounts on the balance sheet.

> **LO 2: Distinguish between debits and credits and apply them to the accounting equation.**

In order to apply these steps, however, some additional information must be used. The accounting system builds on the idea of the equality of assets with liabilities and equity. The accounting equation specifies that assets equal liabilities plus equity. To that equation, a rule is added that says that debits equal credits. Debits mean left, and credits mean right. Assets, which are on the left side of the accounting equation, are designated by debits while liabilities and equity, on the right side of the accounting equation, are designated by credits. Items on the left side of the accounting equation, assets, are increased by debits and decreased by credits. By extension, then, any element which increases items on the right side would carry credit balances while any item which decreases right-side accounts would carry debit balances. Increases in revenues and gains are credits; increases in expenses, losses, and dividends are debits. Debits increase assets, dividends, expenses and losses; they decrease liabilities, equity, revenues, and gains. Credits increase liabilities, equity, revenues, and gains; they decrease assets, dividends, expenses, and losses.

Accounts provide summaries of the activity relating to a specific portion of an accounting element. An example of an account is Cash, the account which summarizes all cash received and all cash spent. Each account has a beginning balance for a period; some items are added to it, and some are subtracted from it. The result each period is an ending balance.

Prior to items being posted to accounts, however, they must be entered into the journal. The journal entry has a specific content which includes the date of the transaction, the accounts affected by the transaction, the amounts by which the accounts change, and other relevant information.

> **LO 3: Identify the normal balance of accounts and distinguish between permanent accounts and temporary accounts.**

Each account has an expected balance, called a normal balance. These are the types of balances expected to appear in the accounts, and are the types of transactions that lead to increases in the account. Assets, dividends, expenses, and losses normally carry debit balances. Liabilities, equity, revenues, and gains normally have credit balances. Entering more of the normal balance into the accounts results in an increase in the account balance; entering the opposite (for example, a credit in a debit-balance account) results in a decrease in the account balance.

The idea of permanent and temporary accounts relates to the accounts which remain on the books as opposed to those that must "start over" each accounting period. The balance sheet accounts, also called permanent accounts, always have a balance and simply increase or decrease during each accounting period. Accounts on the income statement, as well as dividends, must measure activity for specific periods of time. In order to accomplish this goal, the measuring periods must be separated by removing the balances from the accounts each accounting period. Temporarily, each of these accounts has a zero balance at the end of each period.

LO 4: Describe accounts, charts of accounts, journals, ledgers, and worksheets.

Journals record transactions on the approximate date on which they occur. Called the book of original entry, they provide a chronological record of the items that have occurred during the accounting period. To summarize the information about each item, the accountant posts items to the accounts in the **ledger**. This posting brings together the information about specific items in **accounts, such as cash or accounts receivable**. **A chart of accounts** lists each account along with its number so the accountant can locate the account without difficulty. **Worksheets** provide a tool for the accountant to bring together all information from the accounts on a single document in order to determine the accounts that need to be adjusted, to compute the net income to be expected, and to analyze the accounts. The worksheet contains all accounts with balances, adjustments to the accounts, and a calculation of net income and balance sheet totals.

LO 5: Record transactions in journals.

Any journal entry requires that the date of the transaction be entered first. Next, account(s) to be debited is(are) entered and aligned with the left margin of the description column. The balance to be debited to an account is entered into the debit column. Next, any account(s) to be credited is(are) entered in the description column and slightly indented under the debited account. Amounts for credit entry accounts are entered in the credit column. Each entry must contain equal debits and credits. The entry must be posted to the ledger accounts.

LO 6: Post transactions from the general journal to the general ledger.

Posting requires that each entry to each account be recorded in the account bearing the account name. The date of the transaction is entered in the date column, and the journal page on which the entry is found is entered into the posting reference column. The debit or credit amount is entered into the correct column and then is either added or subtracted depending on its relationship with the current balance. If the entries are opposite types of balances, they are netted. If they are the same type of balance, they are added together. The resulting balances are place in the debit or credit column, representing the type of balance they have. The person doing the posting to the ledger must then remember, of course, to go back and post the ledger account number in the journal (as noted in the preceding paragraph).

LO 7: Compute cash discounts and determine the implication of freight terms.

Accounting for merchandise purchased by the company for resale involves several complexities for the accountant. One of the problems is the issue of the amount and date of payment. If cash discounts are available, they are designed to encourage early payment and, therefore, offer a lowered price if the invoice is paid early. The first number in the terms (for example, 2/10, n/30) indicates the percentage of the discount. This percentage, applied to the merchandise total, indicates the dollar amount which can be deducted if the invoice is paid within the time period shown after the slash mark (10 days from invoice date in the above example). If the discount is not taken, the "n" indicates that the full amount, in the example, is due within 30 days of the invoice date.

Freight terms describe an additional area of specialized information. FOB, a term standing for "free on board," indicates the point at which title to the goods transfers from seller to buyer. FOB shipping point states that title transfers to the buyer as soon as the goods are shipped. FOB destination indicates that the seller holds title until the goods arrive at the business of the buyer. Careful attention to these terms is vital to determine whether the seller's inventory or the buyer's inventory should contain the goods. They should be included in the inventory of the entity that holds title. Shipping costs are generally the responsibility of the entity which holds title during shipment.

| LO 8: Prepare a trial balance. | The trial balance provides assurance to the accountant that the debits and credits are equal. The accountant simply lists

each account with its balance in the appropriate debit or credit column. The totals of the columns must equal each other to provide assurance of equality. The accountant must always remember, though, that equal debits and credits are not assurance of correctness.

CHAPTER GLOSSARY

Account: the history of all increases and decreases in an accounting element

Accounting cycle: The sequence of steps repeated in each accounting period to enable the company to analyze, record, classify, and summarize the transactions into financial statements.

Accounting system: a system that gathers data from source transactions to create the books and records that transform the data into a manageable format and eventually produces useful information in the form of financial statements

Accruals: adjustments made to recognize items that should be included in the income statement period but have not yet been recorded

Accrued expense: expense incurred during the financial statement period that has not yet been recognized

Accrued revenue: revenue earned and realizable during the financial statement period that has not yet been recognized or recorded

Bank statement: a summary of the cash inflows and outflows processed by the bank

Chart of accounts: a list of all the accounts used by a business entity

Compound journal entries: journal entries with more than two accounts listed

Cost of goods sold: cost of product sales

Current assets: assets that are likely to be converted to cash or expected to be used within the longer of one year or operating cycle

Current liabilities: debts an entity owes that are expected to be satisfied within one year or one operating cycle with cash, goods, or services

Deferrals: postponements of the recognition of a revenue or expense even though the cash has been received or paid

Deferred expense: an asset created when cash is paid before an expense has been incurred

Deferred revenue: unearned revenue created when cash is received before the revenue is earned

Error corrections: corrections made through adjusting entries when the accountant reviews the trial balance and notices errors in the recording or posting process

FOB point: an old shipping term meaning free on board, which defines the point where title passes and the purchase/sales transaction legally occurs

General journal: a journal for recording all transactions that cannot be recorded in a special journal

General ledger: the entire group of accounts in an accounting system

Intangible assets: assets that give the entity contractual rights

Journal: a book of original entry where a chronology of the business entity's transactions is recorded

Journalizing: the act of recording accounting transactions into a journal

Long-term liabilities: debts owed that are due after one year or one operating cycle

Normal balance: defines the type of entry that increases the account; debits increase debit balance accounts and credits decrease debit balance accounts

Permanent accounts: all asset, liability, and equity accounts, except for the dividend account

Post-closing trial balance: a trial balance prepared after the closing entries are posted to prove that the closing entries zeroed the temporary accounts and the remaining accounts are in balance

Posting: recording each journal transaction into the general ledger account it changes

Posting reference column: a column in the general journal that contains a reference to the general ledger account number affected by each transaction

Property, plant, and equipment: assets expected to have a useful life longer than one year or operating cycle

Retained earnings: total of all earnings of an entity since inception minus all dividends declared

Revenues: amount of equity increased by the normal business activities of the business

Selling expenses: period expenses to market the entity's products

Special journals: journals that record a specific type of transactions such as sales

Stockholders' equity: amounts that represent the ownership interests of the entity

T-account: an abbreviated general ledger account that has only two columns and no explanations

Temporary accounts: all revenue, expense, gain, and loss accounts that are part of net income plus the dividend account

Trial balance: a listing of each general ledger account balance to verify that the general ledger, and therefore the accounting equation, is in balance

Worksheet: a tool accountants use to accumulate the data required to prepare financial statements

PROBLEM APPLICATIONS

Multiple Choice Questions:

For each of the following multiple choice questions, circle the letter of the BEST response.

1. Which of the following contains a partial listing of accounting cycle steps in the proper order?
   A. journalizing, posting, adjusting, preparing the trial balance
   B. posting, adjusting, journalizing, preparing the trial balance
   C. preparing the trial balance, posting, adjusting, journalizing,
   D. journalizing, posting, preparing the trial balance, adjusting

2. A special journal is
   A. A journal which is used to record a specific type of transaction such as sales.
   B. A journal for recording all transactions that cannot be recorded in a specific journal.
   C. A general book of original entry where a chronology of the business entity's transactions is recorded.
   D. A journal for recording only the most important transactions.

3. The posting process includes which of the following?
   A. the journals only
   B. the ledger only
   C. the journals and ledger
   D. the journals, ledger, and financial statements.

4. For accrued expenses, adjustments are necessary to
   A. recognize expenses incurred during the period, but not yet paid
   B. recognize expenses paid during the period, but not yet incurred
   C. adjust the expense and cash accounts
   D. adjust the expense and asset accounts

5. Which of the following accounts would be closed at the end of the year?
   A. Accounts receivable
   B. Inventory
   C. Cost of goods sold
   D. Retained earnings

6. Which of the following lists of accounts contain those that normally have a credit balance?
   A. Liabilities, expenses, and retained earnings
   B. Liabilities, revenues and retained earnings
   C. Assets, liabilities and equity
   D. Assets, dividends and expenses

7. If an invoice dated November first in the amount of $1,000 with terms 3/10, net 30 days, were paid on November seventh, then the payment amount would be
   A. $1,000
   B. $970
   C. $30
   D. $1,030

8. A worksheet is frequently used to help prepare the
   A. journal entries
   B. account balances
   C. trial balance
   D. financial statements

9. The most important step in the accounting cycle is
   A. analysis of transactions.
   B. recording of transactions.
   C. posting to the ledger accounts.
   D. taking the trial balance.

10. The lack of a ledger in an accounting system would result in
    A. more time for the important parts of the system.
    B. difficulty in finding balances of accounts.
    C. faster preparation time for the financial statements.
    D. less need for balanced entries.

True / False Questions:

1. The payment terms 2/10, n/30 indicates that a two percent discount is allowed if payment is made within 10 days of the invoice date; otherwise payment is due 30 days after the invoice date.
2. FOB point is an old shipping terms meaning Free on Board and defines the point at which title passes and the purchase/sale transaction legally occurs.
3. The trial balance guarantees that no errors are present in the accounting data.
4. A revenue accrual would be used to record revenues for services performed, but not yet billed.
5. For deferrals, cash receipt or payment follows recognition of revenue or expense.
6. Every transaction must have at least one debit and one credit.
7. A compound journal entry is a journal entry with more than two accounts listed.
8. Title to goods shipped FOB shipping point would pass when the merchandise leaves the seller's shipping dock.
9. Closing entries eliminate accounts that are no longer needed in the accounting system.
10. Reconciliation of bank statements provide an additional control measure for the system to protect against theft.

Matching:

1. Match each of the following definitions with the item it describes.

_____	1.	accruals	_____ 6.	journal
_____	2.	posting	_____ 7.	permanent accounts
_____	3.	T-account	_____ 8.	deferrals
_____	4.	general ledger	_____ 9.	trial balance
_____	5.	temporary accounts	_____ 10.	normal balance

A. An abbreviated general ledger account with only two columns and no explanations.
B. A book of original entry where chronology of the business entity's transactions are recorded.
C. All revenue, expense, gain, and loss accounts that are part of net income plus the dividend account.
D. Recording each journal transaction into the general ledger account it changes.
E. Postponements of the recognition of a revenue or expense even though the cash has been received or paid.
F. Defines the type of entry that increases the account.
G. The entire group of accounts in an accounting system.
H. A listing of each general ledger account balance to verify that the general ledger, and therefore the accounting equation, is in balance.
I. Adjustments made to recognize items that should be included in the income statement period but have not yet been recorded.
J. All asset, liability, and equity accounts, except for the dividend account.

2. Use the numbers 1 though 8 to identify the order in which the following activities should occur in the accounting cycle.

_____	A.	Prepare financial statements
_____	B.	Take a trial balance
_____	C.	Make adjusting entries
_____	D.	Journalize transactions
_____	E.	Analyze transactions
_____	F.	Prepare and post closing entries
_____	G.	Post journal entries
_____	H.	Prepare post-closing trial balance

Exercises:

1. For each of the following accounts, identify the normal balance and whether the account is temporary or permanent. The first one is done for you as an example.

		Balance	Acct. type
a.	Cash	DR	Perm.
b.	Wages Expense		
c.	Common Stock		
d.	Sales		
e.	Prepaid Rent		
f.	Retained Earnings		
g.	Cost of Goods Sold		
h.	Accounts Receivable		
i.	Accounts Payable		
j.	Equipment		
k.	Dividends		
l.	Rent Expense		
m.	Merchandise Inventory		
n.	Income Tax Expense		
o.	Preferred Stock		
p.	Gasoline Expense		
q.	Supplies Expense		
r.	Rent Revenue		
s.	Mortgage Payable		
t.	Supplies		

2.   Identify each of the accounts below as asset (A), liability (L), Equity (E), Expense (EX), or Revenue (R) for High-Five Company.

_____ 1. Accounts Receivable   _____ 12. Dividends

_____ 2. Common Stock   _____ 13. Accounts Payable

_____ 3. Rent Revenue   _____ 14. Merchandise Inventory

_____ 4. Cost of Goods Sold   _____ 15. Patents

_____ 5. Salaries Expense   _____ 16 Preferred Stock

_____ 6. Retained Earnings   _____ 17. Advertising Expense

_____ 7. Cash   _____ 18. Utilities Expense

_____ 8. Sales   _____ 19. Rent Expense

_____ 9. Prepaid Insurance   _____ 20. Interest Payable

_____ 10. Prepaid Interest   _____ 21. Interest Expense

_____ 11. Interest Revenue   _____ 22. Wages Payable

3.   Using the accounts listed above, prepare a chart of accounts for High-Five Company.

4.   The following invoices were received recently by Cheap, Inc. The company policy is to take all discounts available (of course). For each of the invoices listed below, determine the following:
      1. The date by which the invoice would have to be paid to get the discount.
      2. The amount of the discount.
      3. The net amount to be paid (invoice amount less discount).
      4. The date by which the invoice would have to be paid even without the discount.
A.   Invoice dated July 19, owed to Wilson Brothers, $9,700, terms 1/15, n/30.
B.   Invoice dated July 30, owed to Smith & Jones, Inc., $10,500, terms 2/15, n/30.
C.   Invoice dated August 1, owed to KJ Company, $5,500, terms 3/10, n/ EOM.

5.   For each of the following invoices, determine whether the buyer or seller owns the merchandise on June 9, 2005.
A.   Merchandise shipped 5/30/05, fob destination, received 6/10/05
B.   Merchandise shipped 6/2/05, fob shipping point, received 6/6/05
C.   Merchandise shipped 6/6/05, fob destination, received 6/9/05.

Problems: Work papers in Appendix can be copied for use.

1.   Mid-Semester Company provides tutoring services for students who want (need?) help as mid-term examinations approach. The company had the following transactions during the month of October, 2005.

Oct. 2	Received office supplies on account in the amount of $250.
Oct. 5	Paid wages to employees of $720 (nothing had been recorded earlier.)
Oct. 8	Paid advertising bill of $1,200.
Oct. 9.	Paid $593 on accounts payable.
Oct.10	Paid rent on tutoring site, $500.
Oct.12	Billed students being tutored, $1,200.
Oct. 18	Collected $772 from students who had not been billed.
Oct. 20	Paid utilities, $159.
Oct. 22	Received $950 from students who had been billed for services.
Oct. 30	Paid $120 for supplies for staff.
Oct. 31	Purchased new textbooks to prepare for second semester work, $889.

2.   Assume Mid-Semester Company had the following beginning balances in its accounts:

	Dr.	Cr.
Cash	$6,992	
Accounts Receivable	973	
Office Supplies	505	
Textbooks	703	
Accounts Payable		$ 606
Taxes Payable		1,228
Common Stock		5,000
Retained Earnings		2,339

Instructions:
-   a.   Enter the above amounts into the accounts.
-   b.   Post the transactions journalized in Problem 1 to the accounts.
-   c.   Prepare a trial balance.

3.   For each of the following, determine the probable transaction that gave rise to the journal entry.

1.	Cash	10,000	
	Jones, Capital		10,000
2.	Wages Payable	5,900	
	Cash		5,900
3.	Advertising Expense	1,000	
	Cash		1,000

4.	Merchandise Inventory	5,555	
	Accounts Payable		5,555
5.	Cash	697	
	Sales		697
6.	Gasoline Expense	200	
	Cash		200
7.	Truck	15,000	
	Note Payable		15,000
8.	Utilities Expense	637	
	Cash		637
9.	Notes Payable	12,000	
	Cash		12,000
10.	Training Expense	1,250	
	Cash		1,250

SOLUTIONS

Multiple Choice:

1.	A	6.	B
2.	A	7.	B
3.	C	8.	D
4.	A	9.	A
5.	C	10.	B

True / False:

1. True
2. True
3. False; it only guarantees that the debits are equal to the credits.
4. True
5. False; for deferrals, cash flow occurs before the recognition.
6. True
7. True
8. True

9.   False; closing entries only close temporary accounts (bring the account balances to zero) to prepare them to measure the items for the next accounting period.
10.   True

Matching:

Problem 1

1.	I	6.	B
2.	D	7.	J
3.	A	8.	E
4.	G	9.	H
5.	C	10.	F

Problem 2

A.   6
B.   4
C.   5
D.   2
E.   1
F.   7
G.   3
H.   8

Exercises:

1.
	Account	Balance	Account type
a.	Cash	Dr.	Permanent
b.	Wages Expense	Dr.	Temporary
c.	Common Stock	Cr.	Permanent
d.	Sales	Cr.	Temporary
e.	Prepaid Rent	Dr.	Permanent
f.	Retained Earnings	Cr.	Permanent
g.	Cost of Goods Sold	Dr.	Temporary
h.	Accounts Receivable	Dr.	Permanent
i.	Accounts Payable	Cr.	Permanent
j.	Equipment	Dr.	Permanent
k.	Dividends	Dr.	Temporary
l.	Rent Expense	Dr.	Temporary
m.	Merchandise Inventory	Dr.	Permanent
n.	Income Tax Expense	Dr.	Temporary
o.	Preferred Stock	Cr.	Permanent
p.	Gasoline Expense	Dr.	Temporary

q.	Supplies Expense	Dr.		Temporary
r.	Rent Revenue	Cr.		Temporary
s.	Mortgage Payable	Cr.		Permanent
t.	Supplies	Dr.		Permanent

2.

1.	A	12.	E
2.	E	13.	L
3.	R	14.	A
4.	EX	15.	A
5.	EX	16.	E
6.	E	17.	EX
7.	A	18.	EX
8.	R	19.	EX
9.	A	20.	L
10.	A	21.	EX
11.	R	22	L

3.

High-Five Company
Chart of Accounts

Account Number	Account Name	Classification
101	Cash	Asset
104	Accounts Receivable	Asset
105	Merchandise Inventory	Asset
110	Prepaid Insurance	Asset
114	Prepaid Interest	Asset
180	Patents	Asset
220	Accounts Payable	Liability
230	Wages Payable	Liability
240	Interest Payable	Liability
320	Common Stock	Equity
340	Preferred Stock	Equity
370	Retained Earnings	Equity
390	Dividends	Equity
510	Sales	Revenue
550	Rent Revenue	Revenue
560	Interest Revenue	Revenue
610	Cost of Goods Sold	Expense
620	Salaries Expense	Expense
630	Advertising Expense	Expense

640	Utilities Expense	Expense
650	Rent Expense	Expense
660	Interest Expense	Expense

4.

	Date with discount	Discount amount	Net amount	Date without discount
A.	August 3	$97	$9,603	August 18
B.	August 15	$210	$10,290	August 29
C.	August 11	$165	$5,335	August 30

5.
- A. In transit—belongs to seller
- B. Received—belongs to buyer
- C. Received—belongs to buyer

Problems:

1.

General Journal				Page	1
Date 2005		**Description**	**Post Ref.**	**Debit**	**Credit**
Oct	2	Office Supplies	140	250	
		Accounts Payable	210		250
	5	Wages Expense	610	720	
		Cash	110		720
	8	Advertising Expense	620	1200	
		Cash	110		1200
	9	Accounts Payable	210	593	
		Cash	110		593
	10	Rent Expense	630	500	
		Cash	110		500
	12	Accounts Receivable	120	1200	
		Tutoring Revenue	510		1200
	18	Cash	110	772	
		Tutoring Revenue	510		772
	20	Utilities Expense	640	159	
		Cash	110		159
	22	Cash	110	950	
		Accounts Receivable	120		950
	30	Office Supplies	140	120	
		Cash	110		120
	31	Textbooks	160	889	
		Cash	110		889

Recording Accounting Data

12a and b.

Account Name Cash					Account Number 110		
Date		**Post**			**Balance**		
2005	**Description**	**Ref.**	**Debit**	**Credit**	**Debit**	**Credit**	
Oct 1		J1	6992		6992		
Oct 5		J1		720	6272		
Oct 8		J1		1200	5072		
Oct 9		J1		593	4479		
Oct 10		J1		500	3979		
Oct 18		J1	772		4751		
Oct. 20		J1		159	4592		
Oct 22		J1	950		5542		
Oct 30		J1		120	5422		
Oct 31		J1		889	4533		

Account Name Accounts Receivable					Account Number 120		
Date		**Post**			**Balance**		
2005	**Description**	**Ref.**	**Debit**	**Credit**	**Debit**	**Credit**	
Oct. 1	Beginning Balance	J1	973		973		
Oct.12		J1	1200		2173		
Oct.22		J1		950	1223		

Account Name Office Supplies					Account Number 140		
Date		**Post**			**Balance**		
2005	**Description**	**Ref.**	**Debit**	**Credit**	**Debit**	**Credit**	
Oct. 1		J1	505		505		
Oct. 2		J1	250		755		
Oct. 30		J1	120		875		

Account Name Textbooks					Account Number 160		
Date		**Post**			**Balance**		
2005	**Description**	**Ref.**	**Debit**	**Credit**	**Debit**	**Credit**	
Oct. 1		J1	703		703		
Oct. 31		J1	889		1592		

Account Name	Accounts Payable				Account Number		210
Date		**Post**			**Balance**		
2005	**Description**	**Ref.**	**Debit**	**Credit**	**Debit**	**Credit**	
Oct. 1		J1		606		606	
Oct. 2		J1		250		856	
Oct. 9		J1	593			263	

Account Name	Taxes Payable				Account Number		240
Date		**Post**			**Balance**		
2005	**Description**	**Ref.**	**Debit**	**Credit**	**Debit**	**Credit**	
Oct. 1		J1		1228		1228	

Account Name	Common Stock				Account Number		310
Date		**Post**			**Balance**		
2005	**Description**	**Ref.**	**Debit**	**Credit**	**Debit**	**Credit**	
Oct. 1		J1		5000		5000	

Account Name	Retained Earnings				Account Number		350
Date		**Post**			**Balance**		
2005	**Description**	**Ref.**	**Debit**	**Credit**	**Debit**	**Credit**	
Oct. 1		J1		2339		2339	

Account Name	Tutoring Revenue				Account Number		510
Date		**Post**			**Balance**		
2005	**Description**	**Ref.**	**Debit**	**Credit**	**Debit**	**Credit**	
Oct. 12		J1		1200		1200	
Oct. 18		J1		772		1972	

Account Name	Wages Expense				Account Number		610
Date		Post			Balance		
2005	Description	Ref.	Debit	Credit	Debit	Credit	
Oct. 5		J1	720		720		

Account Name	Advertising Expense				Account Number		620
Date		Post			Balance		
2005	Description	Ref.	Debit	Credit	Debit	Credit	
Oct. 8		J1	1200		1200		

Account Name	Rent Expense				Account Number		630
Date		Post			Balance		
2005	Description	Ref.	Debit	Credit	Debit	Credit	
Oct. 10		J1	500		500		

Account Name	Utilities Expense				Account Number		640
Date		Post			Balance		
2005	Description	Ref.	Debit	Credit	Debit	Credit	
Oct. 20		J1	159		159		

2c.

Mid-Semester Company		
Trial Balance		
October 31, 2005		
	Dr.	Cr.
Cash	$4533	
Accounts Receivable	1223	
Office Supplies	875	
Textbooks	1592	
Accounts Payable		$ 263
Taxes Payable		1228
Common Stock		5000
Retained Earnings		2339
Tutoring Revenue		1972
Wages Expense	720	
Advertising Expense	1200	
Rent Expense	500	
Utilities Expense	159	
Totals	$10802	$10802

3. (1) Owner contributed cash to the business.
    (2) Employees were paid for time worked.
    (3) The company paid for advertising used in the current period.
    (4) The company received merchandise but has not yet paid for it.
    (5) The company recorded sales for cash.
    (6) The company paid for gasoline used this period.
    (7) The company purchased a truck by issuing a note payable.
    (8) The company paid for utilities used this period.
    (9) The company repaid a loan.
    (10) The company paid for one or more employees to receive some specialized training.

Chapter 6
Completing the Accounting Cycle
and Preparing Financial Statements

CHAPTER SUMMARY

<table>
<tr><td>LO 1: Reconcile a bank statement.</td></tr>
</table>

After completion of the trial balance, thereby assuring that the debits equal the credits, the accountant needs to examine the accounts to make sure revenues and expenses are correctly measured. **Reconciling the bank statement to the amount of cash shown in the cash account constitutes a first step in the process.** The bank statement balance and the cash balance need to reconcile to the same amount. The process starts with the balances shown. As a general rule, each entity's balance is adjusted to include items that it had not known about until the other entity's information became available. **The bank, for example, does not know about outstanding checks, deposits in transit, errors, and miscellaneous other items that occur infrequently. The company may not have known about NSF checks, collections by the bank, bank service charges, and errors** until the bank statement was received. When the book cash account balances with the bank statement amount, the **items used to adjust the book balance need to be journalized.** This step provides some assurance that the book balance is correct on the financial statements. Examination of all remaining accounts must now be undertaken.

<table>
<tr><td>LO 2: Adjust the accounts to apply the matching principle</td></tr>
</table>

The **matching principle states that expenses incurred to generate revenues must be matched with those revenues in the period the revenues are earned.** To be sure of finding all of the expenses and revenues we need to recognize, a good procedure is to follow the accounts listed in an orderly progression. The first account we come to after cash is usually the accounts receivable. Accounts receivable lists sales made but not collected. Since not all customers are conscientious about paying accounts, accountants must estimate the amount of receivables that customers will probably not pay. One method of estimating these amounts is through an aging of accounts receivable. As an account becomes older, the likelihood of nonpayment increases. **An entry establishes the potential loss in an account that is subtracted from Accounts Receivable to get the net expected to be collected and to recognize the expense of the non-collection.**

The merchandise inventory account appears next. Since most companies have programs to track items purchased, the beginning inventory plus the amount purchased give the total merchandise that has been available. When the company takes a physical inventory count, the amount left on hand (ending inventory) can be subtracted from the total available to get the amount sold. A journal entry takes goods out of Merchandise Inventory (with a credit) and moves them to Cost of Goods Sold (with a debit).

All inventory accounts act in the same way, and the movement is similar. Manufacturing companies have three different inventory accounts to measure the point at which inventory appears in the system. The movement in inventory accounts can be expressed generically as:

> What you started with
> + What you added
> = Everything available
> - What you have left
> = What has moved on.

The "everything available" amount comes from two places (you started with it, or you added it) and will end in one of two places (you have it left, or it is gone.). This idea translates to manufacturing inventories in the following way:

Raw materials	Work in process	Finished goods
Beginning inventory	Beginning inventory	Beginning inventory
+Purchases	+Direct materials	+ Cost of goods mfgd.
= Total available	+Direct labor	= Total available
- Ending inventory	+ Factory overhead	-Ending inventory
= Cost of items used*	= Total available	= Cost of goods sold
	- Ending inventory	
	= Cost of goods mfgd.	

* These may be direct materials or indirect materials.

The items used from raw materials inventory become input to the work in process, and cost of goods manufactured is input to the finished goods inventory. Even though the **Statement of Cost of Goods Manufactured** takes a somewhat different form for calculations, the basic computation is the one shown above for the work-in-process inventory account. Goods that are transferred out of the finished goods inventory account are treated exactly like Cost of Goods Sold in a merchandising firm. Any inventory account is adjusted by debiting the following inventory or by debiting cost of goods sold for the amount that has moved out of inventory.

Items that have been purchased in advance, such as supplies inventory, prepaid rent, or prepaid insurance, for example, will usually have part of the amount used up during the period. The amount used needs to be computed and taken out of the balance sheet account. The entry is a debit to the related expense account and a credit to the balance sheet account.

Items such as furniture and equipment will depreciate as they are used. These depreciated amounts are debited to depreciation expense, while the credited account is accumulated depreciation, an account that is subtracted from the related asset account on the balance sheet. Depreciation expense may be classified as belonging to selling, administrative, or manufacturing purposes. Amortization expense measures the using up of intangible assets. This calculation is the same as straight-line depreciation but without a salvage value.

On the liabilities side of the balance sheet, any previously unmeasured items that relate to the current period must be recorded as an expense with a corresponding credit to a payable account. These include accounts, interest, payroll taxes, sales taxes, and income taxes, as well as others as relevant to the system being analyzed.

All adjusting entries must include an income statement account (a revenue or an expense) and a balance sheet account (an asset or a liability). Additionally, though correcting entries may use the cash account, adjusting entries will not include cash. When the adjusting entries have been journalized and posted, the accountant is ready to prepare financial statements.

| LO 3: Prepare classified income statements |

The income statement to be prepared follows the format already discussed in Chapter 2. All data for this statement can come from the worksheet columns labeled "income statement." In addition, however, accounting standards require that the earnings per share calculations be included as part of the income statement presentation.

| LO 4: Compute basic earnings per share. |

Earnings per share shows the financial statement user the portion of net income attributable to each share of common stock. In its simplest form, earnings per share is computed as net income divided by the number of common shares of stock outstanding during the period. The "outstanding" portion of the definition means the number of shares being held by investors.

| LO 5: Prepare statements of equity. |

Because the net income figure from the income statement must be used in the statement of stockholders' equity, the income statement had to be completed before the statement of equity. Now, however, the completion of the income statement signals the accountant's ability to construct the statement of equity, again following the format first presented in Chapter 2. Note that all accounts that appear in the equity section of the balance sheet are updated in this statement.

| LO 6: Prepare classified balance sheets |

The completion of the statement of stockholders' equity provides updated information so that the accountant now has available all balances needed to be able to prepare the classified balance sheet. This balance sheet separates the assets held by the company into the Current Asset, the Property, Plant, and Equipment, and the Intangible Assets sections. Liabilities are categorized as Current Liabilities or Long-Term Liabilities. The information from the statement of equity provides the numbers needed for the Stockholders' Equity section of the balance sheet. And again, the total assets equal the total liabilities plus equity.

LO 7: Close the temporary accounts.

At the end of the accounting period, the accounts must be prepared to start the next period. The accounting period may cover any period of time, but cannot exceed a year in length. The company's year need not follow the calendar year; it can follow the natural flow of the business. A business year which differs from the calendar year is called a **fiscal year.** At the end of the year, the business must prepare for the next year. While some accounts continue from period to period with a balance in them, others do not. The balance sheet accounts always have continuing balances. The income statement accounts and dividends, however, measure for a specific period of time, such as the fiscal year. To avoid combining results from two or more periods, the account balances must be brought to zero in order for the measuring to start anew at the beginning of the next period.

To bring the revenue, expense, gain, loss, and dividend accounts to zero, the accountant must enter an offsetting balance into the accounts. The closing entries are four in number. **(1) In the revenue and gain accounts, debit amounts equal to the account balances need to be entered**. The offsetting credit goes to a new account created for just this purpose called Income Summary. Similarly, **(2) the expense and loss accounts are credited with the amount necessary to balance their debit entries, and the Income Summary account is debited. (3) Income Summary is then debited or credited to balance it to zero, and the remaining part of the entry goes to Retained Earnings. (4) The Dividends account is credited for the amount necessary to cause it to balance out, and Retained Earnings is debited.** Note in the example problem presented for you that this process causes all temporary accounts to have a zero balance.

LO 8: Prepare a post-closing trial balance.

The last step in the accounting cycle requires one more check to be sure that debits equal credits. The post-closing trial balance records the balances of all of the balance sheet accounts. Note that the income statement accounts are not included here because their balances have all been eliminated in the closing entries. If any of the temporary accounts do have remaining balances, an error has been made in closing entries and the computation of net income.

CHAPTER GLOSSARY

Aged accounts receivable schedule: a listing of accounts receivable by customer to confirm the total of the receivables and determine the extent to which any accounts are past due

Deposits in transit: deposits recorded in the books that have not been included in the bank statement

Direct labor: the wages of persons who transform direct materials into finished goods

Direct materials: raw materials and purchased components that are measurable in quantity and cost

Earnings per share (EPS): a ratio that reveals how much of a company's net earnings is attributable to each share of common stock

Factory overhead: all other manufacturing costs that are not direct materials or direct labor

Fiscal year: a year that differs from the calendar year but normally coincides with the end of the normal business cycle for its industry

Indirect labor: the cost of supervisory, janitorial, maintenance, security, and other personnel who do not work directly on production but assist direct laborers

Indirect materials: supply items used in manufacturing in small quantities that are impractical to measure

NSF checks: customers' checks that their banks dishonor for insufficient funds and return to the depositor's bank

Outstanding checks: checks that were written through the end of the month but did not appear on the bank statement

Transposition errors: number reversals that cause errors that are always evenly divisible by nine

PROBLEM APPLICATIONS

Multiple Choice:

For each of the following multiple choice questions, circle the letter of the BEST response.

1. Which of the following lists the flow of materials in the correct order?
   A. Raw materials inventory, work-in-process inventory, finished goods inventory, cost of goods sold
   B. Cost of goods sold, raw materials inventory, work-in-process inventory, finished goods inventory
   C. Work-in-process inventory, finished goods inventory, raw materials inventory, goods inventory, cost of goods sold
   D. Finished goods inventory, work-in-process inventory, raw materials inventory, cost of goods sold.

2. If Supplies Inventory had a beginning balance of $800, an ending balance of $500 and $600 of supplies expense was recognized during the period, what was the dollar value of supplies purchased during the period?
   A. $200
   B. $300
   C. $600
   D. $400

3. Which of the following are intangible assets?
   A. Cash
   B. Merchandise Inventory
   C. Patents
   D. Prepaid Insurance

4. Which of the following are adjustments made to the bank statement balance during the reconciliation of the bank account?
   A. Deposits in transit and outstanding checks
   B. Outstanding checks only
   C. Outstanding checks and bank service charges
   D. Bank service charges and NSF checks

5. The need to adjust accounts at the end of the period is most closely related to the
   A. matching principle
   B. full disclosure principle
   C. monetary unit assumption
   D. historical cost principal

6. To calculate earning per share, information is needed from the
   A. Income statement and Balance Sheet
   B. Statement of Cash Flows only
   C. Balance Sheet and Statement of Stockholders' Equity
   D. Income statement and Statement of Cash Flows

7. A classified balance sheet
   A. provides more detailed descriptions of the items listed.
   B. separates items into a variety of sub-categories.
   C. includes additional items normally not found in other statements.
   D. can be completed only at year-end..

8. After reconciliation of the bank account, an entry would need to be entered on the entity's books for
   A. deposits in transit.
   B. errors made by the bank.
   C. customers' NSF checks.

    D. outstanding checks.

9. Manufacturing costs added to work-in-process inventory include
    A. direct materials, indirect materials, and office supplies.
    B. direct labor, indirect labor, and office supplies.
    C. direct materials, office supplies, and executive wages.
    D. direct material, direct labor, and manufacturing overhead

10. The post-closing trial balance
    A. must contain all of the general ledger accounts.
    B. will contain only the permanent accounts that have balances.
    C. may not balance since some of the accounts are excluded.
    D. proves that the closing process has been completed correctly.

True / False:

1. The Statement of Cost of Goods Manufactured simply provides the calculation used to determine the amount added to Finished Goods during the period.
2. Deposits in transit are deducted from the bank statement's ending balance when reconciling the bank account.
3. If the balance in the Merchandise Inventory account differs from the amount of inventory on hand at the end of the period, an error must have been made.
4. The cost of merchandise items used equals beginning inventory plus costs added during the period minus ending inventory.
5. Depreciation Expense and Accumulated Depreciation will usually have the same account balance.
6. Amortization relates to intangible assets like depreciation relates to tangible assets.
7. To comply with GAAP, income statements must disclose the firm's earnings per share.
8. A company's accounting period should end on December 31 of each year.
9. The post-closing trial balances become the opening balances for the new fiscal period.
10. The adjustment process includes accruals, deferrals, and corrections.

Matching:

1.   Match each numbered term with its lettered definition.

_____	1.	deposits in transit	_____ 6.	factory overhead
_____	2.	aged accounts receivable schedule	_____ 7.	outstanding checks
_____	3.	direct materials	_____ 8.	indirect materials
_____	4.	transposition errors	_____ 9.	NSF checks
_____	5.	direct labor	_____ 10.	indirect labor

A   Raw materials and purchased components that are measurable in quantity and cost

B   Number reversals which cause errors that are always divisible by nine.

C   The wage costs of persons who transform direct materials into finished goods.

D   A listing of accounts receivable by customer to confirm the total of the receivables and determine the extent to which any accounts are past due.

E   Deposits recorded in the books that have not been included in the bank statement.

F   Supply items used in manufacturing in small quantities that are impractical to measure.

G   Customers' checks which their banks dishonor for insufficient funds and return to the depositor's bank.

H   Checks which were written through the end of the month but did not appear on the bank statement.

I   Other manufacturing costs that are not direct materials or direct labor.

J   The cost of supervisory, janitorial, maintenance, security and other personnel who do not work directly on production but assist direct laborers.

2. Listed below are the sections of a fully classified balance sheet. Identify the section in which the accounts shown would appear.

A. Current Assets   D. Current Liabilities
B. Property, Plant, & Equipment E. Long-Term Liabilities
C. Intangible Assets   F. Stockholders' Equity

_____ 1. Cash
_____ 2. Automobiles
_____ 3. Accounts Receivable
_____ 4. Prepaid Insurance
_____ 5. Taxes Payable
_____ 6. Long-Term Notes Payable
_____ 7. Building
_____ 8. Short-Term Notes Payable
_____ 9. Rent Payable
_____ 10. Raw Materials Inventory

_____ 11. Retained Earnings
_____ 12. Accounts Payable
_____ 13. Patents
_____ 14. Copyrights
_____ 15. Prepaid Taxes
_____ 16. Merchandise Inventory
_____ 17. Land
_____ 18. Common Stock
_____ 19. Additional Paid-In Capital
_____ 20. Accumulated Depreciation

Exercises: Work papers in Appendix can be copied for use.

1. Brand New, Inc. reported $10,638 in net income for its first year of business. The company had no preferred stock but did have 5,400 shares of common stock outstanding for the entire year. Compute the earnings per share for Brand New.

2. Computer Geeks' new accountant is a bit behind on year-end work. She would like you to record the adjusting entries, as of December 31, 2005, for the following information.

a. A year's worth of insurance was paid on November 1, 2005. The total paid was $7,200. The amount was entered into the Prepaid Insurance account.

b. An aging of accounts receivable indicate that $972 worth of receivables will probably not be collected.

c. The company's only assets are testing equipment for the computers. The equipment cost $8,600 and is expected to last 3 years. Salvage value is expected to be $800. The equipment has been in use for the entire year.

d. The copyright owned by the company was registered at a cost of $5,500. Its expected useful life is five years.

Completing the Accounting Cycle and Preparing the Financial Statements

      e.   Customers' work totaling $782 has been completed, but the customers have not been billed.

      f.   Determine the total effect on net income that would result from these adjusting entries.

Problems:

1. The information below relates to Rothfield, Inc. for its July, 2005, bank reconciliation:

Beginning cash balance per books	$3,000
Deposits-in-transit	150
Interest earned	850
Beginning balance per bank statement	5,510
Bank charge for check printing	20
Outstanding checks	2,000
NSF check	170

Prepare a bank reconciliation for the company and the adjusting journal entry needed as a result.

2. Rollins Company had the following information available:

Raw materials:	Beginning inventory:	$14,770
	Ending inventory:	12,800
Work-in-process:	Beginning inventory	$15,900
	Ending inventory	17,530

The company has purchases of materials of $ 57,500, paid $55,900 in direct labor, and had $165,000 in manufacturing overhead. Prepare the Statement of Cost of Goods Manufactured.

3. Coldwell Company started the month with $647 of supplies; during the month the company purchased $498 in supplies, and at the end of the period the company still had $350 of supplies in hand. Prepare the adjusting journal entry needed for supplies.

4. Below is the adjusted trial balance sheet for Dale Incorporated for the year ended September 30, 2005. Prepare a classified income statement, a statement of retained earnings, and a balance sheet for the company. Do not forget to include the earnings per share, assuming all 302 shares of common stock were outstanding for the entire year.

Worksheet		
Acct # **Account Name**	**Adjusted Trial Balance**	
	Debit	**Credit**
Cash	10,348	
Accounts Receivable	5,200	
Inventory	3,629	
Equipment	42,356	
Land	89,700	
Accounts Payable		6,942
Interest Payable		528
Common Stock		3,020
Additional Paid-in Capital		10,998
Retained Earnings		129,257
Dividends	2,000	
Revenue		50,232
Advertising Expenses	687	
Cost of Goods Sold	40,698	
Interest Expense	209	
Supplies Expense	152	
Wage Expenses	5,998	

5.   Journalize the closing entries for Dale Incorporated (in Problem 4) and   prepare a post-closing trial balance.

SOLUTIONS

Multiple Choice:

1. A	6. A
2. B	7. B
3. C	8. C
4. A	9. D
5. A	10. B

Completing the Accounting Cycle and Preparing the Financial Statements

True / False:
1. True
2. False; deposits in transit are added to the bank statement's ending balance when reconciling the bank account.
3. False; if the balance in the Merchandise Inventory account differs from the amount of inventory on hand at the end of the period, those items that are gone are presumed sold.
4. True
5. False; other than at the end of the first year, Accumulated Depreciation and Depreciation Expense will usually have different account balances because the Depreciation Expense account is closed each year and Accumulated Depreciation is not.
6. True
7. True
8. False; a company may choose a fiscal year which coincides with the end of the normal business cycle for its industry.
9. True
10. True

Matching:

1.

1.	E.
2.	D
3.	A
4.	B
5.	C
6.	I
7.	H
8.	F
9.	G
10.	j

2.

1.	A	11.	F
2.	B	12.	D
3.	A	13.	C
4.	A	14.	C
5.	D	15.	A
6.	E	16.	A
7.	B	17.	B
8.	D	18.	F
9.	D	19.	F
10.	A	20.	B

Exercises:

1. $10,638 \div 5,400 = 1.97 / share

2. a. Insurance Expense   1,200
            Prepaid Insurance   1,200

    b. Doubtful Account Expense   972
            Allowance for Doubtful Accounts   972

c. Depreciation Expense   2,600
     Accumulated Depreciation   2,600

($8,600 – 800) ÷ 3 = $2,600 per year

d. Amortization Expense   1,100
     Copyright   1,100

$5,500 ÷ 5 = $1,100 per year

e. Accounts Receivable   782
     Service Revenue   782

f. (1,200)
   (972)
   (2,600)
   (1,100)
     782
$(5,090) reduction in net income.

Problems:

1.

Rothfield, Inc.
Bank Reconciliation
July

Balance per Bank Statement	5,510
Add: Deposits in Transit	150
Deduct: Outstanding Checks	2,000
Corrected Bank Balance	3,660
Balance per Books	3,000
Add: Interest earned	850
Deduct: NSF check	170
Bank charges	20
Corrected Book Balance	3,660

July 31	Cash	660	
	Accounts Receivable	170	
	Service Charge Expense	20	
	Interest Revenue		850

2.

Direct Materials

Beginning raw material inventory	14,770
Add: Purchases	57,500
Direct material available for use	72,270
Less: Ending inventory	12,800
Direct materials used	59,470
Direct Labor	55,900
Manufacturing Overhead	165,000
Total costs transferred to Work-in-Process	280,370
Add: Beginning Work-in-Process Inventory	15,900
Total Work-in-Process	296,270
Less: Ending Work-in-Process Inventory	17,530
Total Cost of Goods Manufactured	278,740

3.

Supplies Expense	795	
Supplies		795

Starting balance	647
Supplies added	498
Total available	1145
Supplies left	350
Supplies used	795

4.

Dale Incorporated
Income Statement
For the year ended September 30, 2005

Revenue	$50,232	
Cost of goods sold	40,698	
Gross profit		$9,534
Expenses:		
Advertising Expense	$ 687	
Supplies Expense	152	
Wages Expense	5,998	
Interest Expense	209	
Total Expenses		7,046
Net Income		$2,488

Earnings per share: $2,488 \div 302 = \$8.24$ per share

Dale Incorporated
Statement of Retained Earnings
For the year ended September 30, 2005

Retained Earnings, October 1, 2004	$129,257
+ Net income	2,488
Subtotal	$131,745
- Dividends	(2,000)
Retained Earnings, September 30, 2005	$129,745

Completing the Accounting Cycle and Preparing the Financial Statements

Dale Incorporated
Balance Sheet
September 30, 2005

Assets			Liabilities and Equity		
Current Assets:			Liabilities:		
Cash	$10,348		Accounts Payable	$6,942	
Accounts Receivable	5,200		Interest Payable	528	
Inventory	3,629		Total Liabilities		$7,470
Total Current Assets	$19,177				
			Equity:		
Property, Plant, & Equipment:			Common Stock	$ 3,020	
Equipment	$42,356		Additional Paid-In		
Land	89,700		Capital	10,998	
Total PP & E		$122,056	Retained Earnings	129,745	
			Total Equity		143,763
Total Assets		$151,233	Total Liabilities & Equity		$151,233

5.	Revenue	50,232		
	Income Summary		50,232	
	Income Summary	47,744		
	Cost of Goods Sold		40,698	
	Advertising Expense		687	
	Supplies Expense		152	
	Wages Expense		5,998	
	Interest Expense		209	
	Income Summary	2,448		
	Retained Earnings		2,448	
	Retained Earnings	2,000		
	Dividends		2,000	

Dale Incorporated
Post-Closing Trial Balance
September 30, 2005

	Dr.	Cr.
Cash	$10,348	
Accounts Receivable	5,200	
Inventory	3,629	
Equipment	42,356	
Land	89,700	
Accounts Payable		$ 6,942
Interest Payable		528
Common Stock		3,020
Additional Paid-In Capital		10,998
Retained Earnings		129,745
Totals	$151,233	$151,233

Chapter 7
Using Analytical Review
for Internal Financial Decisions
and Planning for Cash

CHAPTER SUMMARY

LO 1: Identify the internal users of analytical review techniques and the types of decision information the techniques provide.

Many individuals and entities utilize financial analysis in making decisions about companies. However, internal decision-makers, those who are making decisions for the companies, are among the most influential users of the information. In addition to simply using the statements, managers must shoulder the responsibility for **representational faithfulness.** Because managers also use the financial statements in analyzing trends of the business and managing cash flow, they have an interest in assuring that these statements are accurate. Managers rely on the financial statement analyses to make decisions about financing of the business and directing its activities.

LO 2: Distinguish between trend analysis and common-size statement techniques.

Two basic types of analysis which are useful for all forms of business are the trend analysis and common-size statement analysis. The **trend analysis** examines changes over time in a business. As a horizontal analysis, it gives the analyst a historical perspective of the direction in which key financial data have been moving over time. A **common-size statement** analysis takes a different perspective, that of the relationships among financial statement items within a given accounting period. This vertical analysis avoids the problems of company size by converting all dollar figures to percentages of important totals on the statements. This technique makes comparisons of numbers on the statements easier to understand. Income statement numbers are converted to percentages of net sales, while balance sheet numbers become percentages of total assets. The conversion to percentages also makes comparisons among companies easier.

Limitations do exist in analysts' ability to utilize these techniques. First, the context of the information must be considered. While the numbers will give a true picture of the status of the company, the analyst must remember that these numbers are impacted by external events, such as the general economy, the economy within the specific industry, and changes of management. Additionally, the analyst must always remember that the information being analyzed is historical data. The decisions being made are attempting to predict; thus, the effects of changes between the past and future must be included in the analysis.

LO 3: Perform analytical reviews in the forms of trend analysis and common-size statements.

The selection of a base year for the **trend analysis** provides a starting point for the review. When the amount of a given account balance is divided by itself, of course, the result is 100%, denoted in the analysis as 100. **Each succeeding year continues to be divided by that same base year amount** so the analyst can see whether the item is increasing, decreasing, or staying constant. The technique allows the analyst to examine any items of interest, such as changes in total assets, comparative changes in specific assets, or comparative changes in assets, liabilities, and equity on the **balance sheets**, as well as any other items the analyst chooses to examine.

A comparable analysis can be applied to the **income statement** items to determine the direction in which these items are trending. The analyst can determine the growth or decline in sales, cost of goods sold, expenses, or net income, for example. Additionally, the results can be shown in graph form for a pictorial view of the results discovered. Earnings per share on the income statement can also by analyzed through the trend analysis technique.

The **statement of cash flows**, when analyzed by trend analysis, clearly shows trends in cash results. Such important questions as whether operating cash flows have been positive and increasing and how cash flow from operating activities compares to cash flows in the other sections of the cash flow statement can be answered and shown through graphs to get a good perspective on trends.

A **common-size statement analysis** allows for comparative analysis within a given accounting period. Creation of the **common-size balance sheet** requires dividing each balance sheet item by the total assets. This calculation yields percentages which can be added or subtracted in the same manner as the dollar figures on the balance sheet. All asset percentages should sum to 100% as should all liability plus equity percentages. Questions to be answered through this analysis included the appropriateness of the asset composition or the degree of risk incurred by the capital structure of the firm. Risk increases with an excess of debt percentage over equity percentage.

The **common-size income statement** requires dividing each item on the income statement by net sales. Again, the percentages found through the conversion will add and subtract exactly like the dollar figures from which the percentages have been derived. That is, sales percentage less cost of goods sold percentage results in the gross margin percentage. By viewing the percentages across time, the analyst can also get a good perspective on the shifts within the statement. For example, is cost of goods sold becoming a more important figure year after year? If so, the company should probably be raising prices on goods sold or finding ways to cut merchandise costs.

LO 4: Prepare a cash flow statement.

An additional statement must be considered to have all information available about a given company. The **statement of cash flows** offers an entirely different perspective on the company. Prior to 1989, this statement was not required. During the years before the cash flow statement requirement, information about cash flows could easily be overlooked in company analysis. The nature of financial accounting and the manner of measuring revenues and expenses does not focus on the receipt or payment of cash. Yet adequate cash inflows are vital to the health of any business. Thus, the inclusion of this statement contributed valuable information to the financial statement analyst. From the statement, the financial analyst could **assess the company's ability to generate positive future net cash flows, assess the company's need for external financing and its ability to pay debts and dividends, assess a company's overall financial health, and reconcile the differences between net income and the change in cash.** The statement is presented in three sections, each showing cash flows of a distinct activity of the business.

The **operating activities** section of the cash flow statement uses the information found on the income statement but converts the information to a cash measurement by examining the changes in current asset and current liability accounts. Inflows come from generation of revenues through sales, dividends received, and interest received. If, however, any receivables account has increased, that increase means that the company did not get the money so that increase would need to be subtracted to get cash inflows; decreases in accounts receivable mean additional cash inflows. Additionally, if any unearned revenue account increased, that increase indicates that the company got money but has not earned the revenue so the increase would need to be added; a decrease means the item is counted as a revenue, but no cash was received during the current period. That decrease would need to be subtracted.

Operating outflows are reflected in the expenses accountants recognize to generate the revenues. Items such as cost of goods sold, insurance expense, tax expense, and so forth must be paid by cash. If, however, any payable accounts have increased, those represent cash not spent; a decrease in them indicates additional cash outflow. An increase in a prepaid account, like prepaid insurance, means extra cash was paid; a decrease indicates the use of something paid for in another period. Overall, the company should experience net cash inflows from operating activities. Otherwise, the company will not be able to stay in business.

Investing activities, the second section of the statement of cash flows, looks at changes in long term assets. These long-term assets are the areas in which the company has invested money in order to be able to conduct business operations. Increases in items like automobiles, buildings, investments in other companies, or intangible assets require the payment (outflow) of cash. This outflow of cash indicates the company is growing and is desirable. The only inflows of cash in this category come from sale of these long-term assets. If a company has a net cash inflow in investing activities, the company is probably in trouble or going out of business.

The third section of the statement of cash flows is the **financing activities** section. Financing for a business comes from sale of stock of the business or borrowing of funds from banks or other types of lending entities. Thus, the long-term liabilities and equity sections of the balance sheet provide the information for use in this section. Cash being borrowed or cash coming into the business from sale of stock represents cash inflow. Repayment of debt, purchase of treasury stock, and payment of dividends to stockholders represent outflows of cash. The net cash flow may be either positive or negative in this section.

One additional consideration complicates the life of the preparer of the statement of cash flows. FASB allows two different methods for preparation of the operating activities section. Both the **direct method** and the **indirect method** are acceptable for financial reporting. Most companies use the indirect method simply because it requires less work. However, since both methods are acceptable and may be encountered in financial statement analysis, the dedicated student will study and understand both techniques.

The actual preparation of the statement requires the use of an income statement and the balance sheets representing (1) the start of the period covered by the income statement and (2) the end of the period covered by the income statement. These statements will allow the preparer of the statement to see the results of operations (the income statement) and to be able to compute the changes that have occurred in all accounts on the balance sheets during the time covered by the income statement.

The **direct method** of preparing the **operating activities** section converts income statement items to cash. For example, the sales revenue must be adjusted to represent additional cash from declines in accounts receivable or to show lack of cash indicated by an increase in accounts receivable. Cost of goods sold is adjusted for changes in inventory and accounts payable to yield cash paid for merchandise. Other items on the income statement require similar adjustments to determine the actual cash flow.

The **indirect method** also requires two balance sheets and the income statement representing the period between them. This calculation, however, starts with the net income on the income statement. Next, the income is increased for items that have reduced net income but have not required the use of cash. These items include depreciation expense, amortization expense, and losses. If the income statement contains gains, these need to be subtracted out because they will be used in the other parts of the statement. This method also requires the disclosure of cash paid for interest and taxes at the bottom of the statement.

Next, adjustments must be made for changes in current asset and current liability accounts (except for Notes Receivable and Notes Payable, of course). The easiest way to correctly make these adjustments utilizes the rules you know for debit and credit effects on the accounts. Asset accounts increase with a debit and decrease with a credit; liability accounts increase with a credit and decrease with a debit. The adjustments to net income for changes in these current accounts require that debit changes to accounts be subtracted from net income while credit changes are added to net income.

The **investing activities** section provides a break from the complexity of the operating activities section. Only one format can be used, and the adjustments are straight-forward. Any increase in a long-term asset account or in Notes Receivable, regardless of classification, means that cash has been expended. Decreases in cash indicate inflows of cash. An important point to remember on the sale of long-term assets is that you are recording actual cash received in this section, not just the book value of the asset. You may need to check the income statement to see if gains or losses have been recorded so you can determine the actual cash received on the sale of the asset. Over time, of course, a healthy business will want to see a net cash outflow in investing activities since such a result indicates the business is growing.

Financing activities relate to Notes Payable, regardless of classification, long-term liability, and equity changes. Increases in these accounts mean that cash has either come into the company or been saved by the company while decreases require that cash be spent.

Adding increases to cash and subtracting decreases to cash will yield the change in cash for the period. The addition of the beginning cash balance (or the netted amount if you have a net decrease) will yield the ending cash balance. The only remaining requirements are for schedules of interest and taxes paid and the schedule of non-cash transactions if these exist.

LO 5: Analyze the information provided on a cash flow statement.

Information on the statement of cash flows indicates the method by which the company is financing its activities. Initially, all companies utilize financing to support their investing. Within a relatively short period of time, all companies need to be able to generate enough cash from operating activities to support the business and acquire additional needed assets. A company which is showing negative cash flows from operations and positive cash flows from investing and financing probably is in trouble. Only operating activities can consistently provide positive cash flows while the company is growing stronger.

LO 6: Compute cash ratios and describe the decision information provided by cash

Several ratios can provide the manager with tools to understand the evidence provided by the statement of cash flows. **Cash to total assets** (cash divided by total assets) provides a measure of the portion of total assets represented by cash. A company wants enough cash on hand to pay the bills, but too much cash indicates an idle resource. Money should be working for the company and helping to generate more money!

Free cash flows (Operating cash flows minus capital expenditures and dividends) provide a measure of cash available for special projects. It indicates how much cash is left over after providing for those items the company MUST fund, such as operations, capital expenditures, and dividends to stockholders.

Adequacy of support for operations can be measured by the next calculations. **Operating cash flow divided by average current liabilities** indicates the degree of comfort a company has in its ability to pay current liabilities as they come due. If the calculation yields a number of one or less, managers will know that the company can barely pay current debts. Additional expenditures should probably be avoided unless the situation is a short-term problem. The last formula, **operating cash flow divided by average total liabilities** measures the company's ability to pay all debts from current operations. Few companies can achieve this goal, but those that do are extremely strong and can expand operations if they desire.

LO 7: Describe the importance of cash management.

Cash management constitutes one of the most important aspects of good company management. A company that runs out of cash, especially if the problem were not anticipated, will have serious results for the business. The company will be unable to grow, it will be unable to acquire goods for sale since suppliers will find lack of payment offensive, and employees will leave if they are not paid. Lenders and investors have limits as to the degree to which they will continue to contribute money to a company that does not seem to be viable. Overall, cash management constitutes one of the most important duties of any company's management team.

CHAPTER GLOSSARY

Analytical review techniques: tools financial analysts use to identify relationships among financial data

Cash to total assets ratio: a ratio that measures the percentage of total assets made up of cash

Common-size statement: an analysis that converts each element of the balance sheet from dollar amounts to percentages of total assets and each element of an income statement from dollar amounts to percentages of sales

Direct method: a method of preparing the operating section of the cash flow statement that presents the amount of cash inflows from customers, interest earned on loans, and dividends received and the cash outflows for merchandise, wages, operating expenses, taxes, and interest

Financing activities: activities that involve the borrowing and repayment of cash and changes in equity from owners' transactions

Free cash flows: the operating cash flows remaining after capital expenditures and dividends

Indirect method: a method of preparing the operating section of the cash flow statement that begins with net income and adjusts it for all items that did not generate or use cash

Investing activities: activities that provide the resources that support operations

Operating activities: activities centered around the company's primary business activities

Operating cash flows to average current liabilities ratio: a ratio that measures the ability to pay current debt from operating cash flows

Operating cash flows to average total liabilities ratio: a ratio that measures the ability to pay total debt from operating cash flows

Supply-chain management: the business process of ordering, handling, and managing inventory

Trend analysis: a technique that indicates the amount of changes in key financial data over time

PROBLEM APPLICATIONS

Multiple Choice Questions:

Multiple Choice Questions: For each of the following multiple choice questions, circle the letter of the BEST response.

1. Which of the following questions could be answered with the financial results from one year only?
   a. Did assets, liabilities and stockholders' equity grow at the same rate?
   b. Has the net income percentage increased or decreased over time?
   c. Did EPS rise in proportion to the increase in sales?
   d. What is the composition of assets?

2. The statement of cash flows helps assess
   a. A company's growth rate.
   b. A company's need to sell additional stock.
   c. A company's profitability.
   d. A company's ability to generate cash flows.

3. Financing activities cash flows would include the purchase of
   a. inventory.
   b. equipment.
   c. treasury stock.
   d. prepaid insurance.

4. Which of the following statements is correct regarding the statement of cash flows?
   a. The direct method will produce a more accurate calculation of cash flows from operating activities than the indirect method.
   b. The indirect method will produce a more accurate calculation of cash flows from operating activities than the direct method.
   c. The direct method begins with net income and adjusts it for all items that did not use or generate cash.
   d. The direct method presents the amount of cash inflows from customers and adjusts it for all items that did not use or generate cash.

5. A cash outflow from an operating activity would include
   a. payments received from customers.
   b. payments made to employees
   c. payments made to purchase equipment
   d. payments received from the sale of equipment.

6. What are the sections that make up the statement of cash flows?
   a. Operating, investing and financing.
   b. Liquidity, profitability and solvency.
   c. Assets, liabilities and equity.
   d. Inflows, outflows, and net.

7. On the statement of cash flows, depreciation expense would
   a. appear or not, depending on the method used.
   b. reduce the financing section.
   c. reduce the investing section.
   d. reduce the operating section.

8. In preparing a statement of cash flows, which of the following would be considered an investing activity?
   a. Discarding of a piece of fully depreciated equipment.
   b. Paying employee wages.
   c. Issuing bonds at a premium.
   d. Lending money to a supplier.

9. Calculation of free cash flow yields the amount of money
   a. on which no interest must be paid.
   b. available to apply toward strategic goals.
   c. to be used for payment of current liabilities.
   d. available for payment of dividends to shareholders.

10. An increase in Accounts Receivable would appear in the statement of cash flows as
    a. an increase in operating cash flows.
    b. a decrease in operating cash flows.
    c. an increase in investing cash flows.
    d. a decrease in investing cash flows.

True/False Questions:

1. Trend analysis is a technique that converts each element of the balance sheet from a dollar amount to a percentage of total assets and each element of an income statement from a dollar amount to a percentage of sales.
2. A limitation of analytical review analysis is that our ability to predict the future using past results depends upon the predictive value of the information we use.
3. A strength of analytical review analysis is the financial statements used for analysis are based on historical cost.
4. A question that could be answered by reviewing a trend analysis of the balance sheet is, "Did each component of assets grow at the same rate as total assets?"
5. A more aggressive debt structure indicates a higher risk.
6. Normally, steady asset growth indicates a positive direction for a company.
7. For a merchandising firm, the key factor to increasing profits is maintaining or increasing the cost of sales.
8. A company cannot logically sell assets it needs to run its operations because then cash generated through operating activities would eventually cease.
9. The change in cash should equal the change in equity from year to year.
10. Depreciation and amortization should be added to net income when preparing the operating section of the statement of cash flows.
11. The Financial Accounting Standards Board requires that a statement of cash flows be prepared using the direct method of computing cash flows from operating activities.
12. A well-managed company will have enough cash on hand to pay the coming year's liabilities.

Using Analytical Review for Internal Financing Decisions
and Planning for Cash

Matching: Match each item below to the correct letter of the definition that follows.

1.   Definitions

_____ 1. Common-size statement   _____ 6. Financing activities

_____ 2. Cash to total assets ratio   _____ 7. Operating cash flows
                                                        to average total liabilities

_____ 3. Operating activities   _____ 8. Investing activities

_____ 4. Supply-chain management   _____ 9. Free cash flows

_____ 5. Operating cash flows to   _____ 10. Trend analysis
            average current liabilities

A.   The business process of ordering, handling, and managing inventory
B.   A technique that indicates the amount of changes in key financial data over time.
C.   Activities centered around the company's primary business activities.
D.   A measure of the percentage of total assets comprised of cash.
E.   A measure of the ability to pay current debt from operating cash flows.
F.   An analysis that converts each element of the balance sheet from dollar amounts
     to percentages of total assets and each element of an income statement from dollar
     amounts to percentages of sales.
G.   Activities that relate to the sale of equity or borrowing from lenders.
H.   Operating cash flows remaining after capital expenditures and dividends.
I.   Activities that provide resources that support operations.
J.   A measure of the ability to pay total debt from operating cash flows.

2. Indicate whether each of the following items are operating (O), investing (I), or financing (F) activities. If the item is not a cash flow item, indicate by inserting N in the space.

_____ 1. Customers paid on their accounts

_____ 2. XYZ bought treasury stock

_____ 3. XYZ bought inventory on account

_____ 4. XYZ sold machinery for book value

_____ 5. Bank loaned XYZ $50,000

_____ 6. XYZ sold stock

_____ 7. XYZ signed a note to purchase a building

_____ 8. XYZ paid for insurance that will be used next year

_____ 9. XYZ used advertising that had been paid last month

_____ 10. Employees were paid for time worked

_____ 11. Supplier sent a bill for freight charges

_____ 12. An employee was given an advance on wages

_____ 13. XYZ declared dividends

_____ 14. XYZ paid dividends

_____ 15. XYZ received dividends on an investment in ABC

Using Analytical Review for Internal Financing Decisions
and Planning for Cash

Exercises:

1. You are given the following income statement for Gnu Company. In the space
    beside the statement, enter the common-size amounts.

Gnu Company
Income Statement
For the Year Ended June 30, 2005

Sales		$97,483
Cost of Goods Sold		43,200
Gross Profit		$54,283
Expenses:		
Wages	$23,665	
Depreciation	15,808	
Utilities	2,335	
Insurance	7,902	
Total expenses		49,710
Net Income		$ 4,573

2. The Farrow Company reported the financial information below:

	2003	**2002**	**2001**
Revenue	67,716	59,400	54,000
Cost of Goods Sold	56,125	48,384	43,200
Gross Profit	11,591	11,016	10,800
Less Expenses			
Selling, General and			
Administrative	4,752	4,400	4,000
Net Income	2,566	2,748	3,200

Prepare a trend analysis for the items presented and comment on your findings.

3. The Bauer Company reported the financial information below:

	2003	**2002**
Assets		
Cash	96,854	121,067
Accounts Receivable	394,235	246,397
Inventory	153,936	102,624
Total Current Assets	645,025	470,088
Noncurrent Assets	1,435,700	1,150,905
Total Assets	2,080,725	1,620,993

Prepare a common size analysis for the assets and comment on your findings.

Using Analytical Review for Internal Financing Decisions
and Planning for Cash

4. The following information is available for the McKinney Company:

Revenue	56,000
Expenses	
Cost of Goods Sold	41,500
Wages	6,000
Depreciation	3,200
Taxes	1,450
Net Income	3,850
Decrease in accounts receivable	2,000
Purchase of equipment	5,000
Increase in accounts payable	3,000

Prepare the operating section of the company's statement of cash flows.

5.   Jensen Company presented the following results in its statement of cash flows for the year just ended.

Cash flow from Operating Activities	$(48,000)
Cash flow from Investing Activities	(15,000)
Cash flow from Financing Activities	90,000
Change in cash balance	$27,000

What do you think might have caused the type of results shown here?

Problems:

1.   The comparative balance sheets of the Bowden Corporation are below:

	2003	2002
Assets		
Cash	3,530	5,681
Accounts Receivable	11,605	12,453
Inventory	47,800	43,025
Property and Equipment, net	97,800	89,412
Total Assets	160,735	150,571
Liabilities and Stockholders' Equity		
Account Payable	14,092	12,394
Wages Payable	2,350	3,102
Bonds Payable	56,031	49,613
Common Stock	500	450
Additional Paid-in Capital	37,500	33,750
Retained Earnings	50,262	51,262
Total Liabilities and Stockholders' Equity	160,735	150,571

During 2003, the company incurred a net loss of $1,000 after incurring operating expenses which included depreciation expense of $2,400; the company paid no dividends during the year. The company also purchased $10,788 of equipment during the period and made no sales of equipment.

Prepare the company's statement of cash flows for 2003, using the indirect method for operating activities.

2.   You are given selected information from the financial statements of Executives, Inc.

Total current assets	$597,282	Average current assets	$696,585
Total assets	993,484	Average total assets	984,909
Total current liabilities	104,607	Average current liabilities	152,404
Total liabilities	545,600	Average total liabilities	602,300
Capital expenditures	175,900	Cash	290,500
Dividends	24,000		
Cash provided by operating activities			389,703

Calculate the following for Executives, Inc. and explain what each calculation tells you.

a.   Cash to total assets:

b.   Operating cash flows to average current liabilities ratio:

c.   Operating cash flows to average total liabilities ratio:

SOLUTIONS

Multiple Choice Questions:

1. D   6. A
2. D   7. A
3. C   8. D
4. D   9. B
5. B   10. B

True / False Questions:

1. False; common-size analysis is a technique that converts each element of the balance sheet from dollar amounts to percentages of total assets and each element of an income statement from dollar amounts to percentages of sales.
2. True
3. False; the fact that financial statements used for analysis are based on historical cost is a limitation of analytical review.

4. True
5. True
6. True
7. False; for a merchandising firm, a key factor to increasing profits is maintaining or decreasing the cost of sales.
8. True
9. False; the change in cash should equal the change in liabilities plus the change in equity plus the change in assets other than cash. Cash and equity are measuring two different items.
10. True
11. False; the Financial Accounting Standards board allows either the direct or indirect method of presenting cash flows from operating activities.
12. False; holding enough cash for an entire year's liability payments would create a high balance of idle cash; cash should be working for the company.

Matching:

1.   Definitions:

1.	F	6.	G
2.	D	7.	J
3.	C	8.	I
4.	A	9.	H
5.	E	10.	B

2.   Cash flow statement sections:

1.	O	8	O
2.	F	9.	N
3.	N	10.	O
4.	I	11.	N
5.	F	12.	O
6.	F	13.	N
7.	N	14.	F
8.	O	15.	O

Using Analytical Review for Internal Financing Decisions
and Planning for Cash

Exercises:

1.

Gnu Company
Income Statement
For the Year Ended June 30, 2005

Sales	$97,483	100.00%
Cost of Goods Sold	43,200	44.32%
Gross Profit	$54,283	55.68%
Expenses:		
Wages	$23,665	24.28%
Depreciation	15,808	16.21%*
Utilities	2,335	2.40%
Insurance	7,902	8.10%*
Total expenses	49,710	50.99%
Net Income	$ 4,573	4.69%

*These percentages have been rounded down to allow correct addition and subtraction of income statement percentages. Carrying the percentages out to more places would eliminate the problem of needing to round down.

2.

	2003	2002	2001
Revenue	125%	110%	100%
Cost of Goods Sold	130%	112%	100%
Gross Profit	107%	102%	100%
Less Expenses			
Selling, General and			
Administrative	119%	110%	100%
Net Income	80%	86%	100%

Although the company's revenue has improved, its cost of goods sold has increased at a faster rate. Additionally, the company's expenses grew at the same rate as sales in 2002 and nearly the same rate in 2003. As a result, the company's net income decreased relative to the base year of 2001. The company needs to focus on ways to reduce costs of both products being sold and general expenses.

3.

	2003	**2002**
Assets		
Cash	4.7%	7.5%
Accounts Receivable	18.9%	15.2%
Inventory	7.4%	6.3%
Total Current Assets	31.0%	29.0%

The company sales appear to have been made on account more often than on a cash basis because Cash is a smaller percentage of total assets in 2003 than in 2002 and accounts receivable comprises a larger percentage of total assets during the same period. Inventory also is a larger component of total assets in 2003 versus 2002. As a result, total current assets grew as a percentage of total assets. The company needs to be cautious since a growth in inventory and in accounts receivable often indicates a slowdown in the general economy because sales slow and more customers charge their purchases instead of paying cash. Additional information could be determined by also examining sales and cost of goods sold amounts.

4.

Net Income	3,850
Adjustments	
Add Depreciation	3,200
Add Decrease in accounts receivable	2,000
Add Increase in accounts payable	3,000
Net Cash Flow from Operating Activities	12,050

5.

The observed results could well have occurred if Jensen were a fairly new company. When companies begin, they often must finance through sales of stock or borrowing and spend money on long-term assets. Another fairly common result of their "newness" appears as negative operating outcomes for a short period of time. Over time, then, the business becomes more established and the firm is able to provide internal financing through profitable operations. We then start to see the more normal patterns of a profitable, on-going business.

Problems:

1.

Bowden Corporation
Statement of Cash Flows
for the period ending 2003

Cash Flows from Operating Activities	
Net Income	(1,000)
Adjustments	
Depreciation expense	2,400
Increase in Accounts Receivable	848
Decrease in Inventory	(4,775)
Increase in Accounts Payable	1,698
Decrease in Wages Payable	(752)
Net Cash Provided by Operating Activities	(1,581)
Cash Flows from Investing Activities	
Purchase of Equipment	(10,788)
Net Cash Used by Investing Activities	(10,788)
Cash Flows from Financing Activities	
Issuance of Bonds Payable	6,418
Sale of common stock	3,800
Payment of dividends	
Net Cash Used by Financing Activities	10,218
Net Change in Cash	(2,151)
Beginning Cash balance	5,681
Ending Cash balance	3,530

2.   a.   .2924 to 1.

Cash comprises approximately 30% of total assets.

      b.   2.557 to 1

Operating cash flows are approximately 2.5 times the average current liabilities. The company can pay average current liabilities 2.5 times with its operating cash flows.

c.   .647 to 1

Operating cash flows are slightly under 65% of total liabilities. The
company is not generating enough cash flows through operations to be
able to pay more than approximately 65% of its total liabilities.

Chapter 8
Analyzing Financial Statements
for Profitability, Liquidity, and Solvency

CHAPTER SUMMARY

An examination of a company's financial statements provides the initial insight into the financial health and management of the firm. To achieve a deeper level of understanding, however, the dedicated analyst should perform financial statement analysis. In addition to trend analysis and common-size statements, a number of formulas provide the analyst with tools to examine relationships among the items on the statements. These tools need to be applied in conjunction with information about the economic and political environment in which the entity operates.

In this chapter, the focus is on utilizing ratio analysis to extend our knowledge of companies. However, just calculating the ratios themselves will add little value to the financial statement information. Instead, the careful and knowledgeable interpretation and analysis produce the value-added component of ratios. Additionally, the analyst greatly extends the value of ratio analysis by comparing individual firms with others in the same industry. In general, ratios provide analysts with information on the profitability, liquidity, or solvency of the company or companies being examined.

> **LO 1: Distinguish among profitability, liquidity, and solvency.**

The areas of profitability, liquidity, and solvency comprise three vital components of management. **Profitability** describes how easily the company generates income. To be profitable, a company must utilize the assets it owns to provide products or services or both to customers at a price above its cost. Since profitability depends on achieving sales prices above cost, this aspect of analysis utilizes the firm's sales and net income.

Liquidity ratios examine the ease with which the assets of the firm are converted to cash. In general, the focus is on short-term obligations since, if an entity cannot meet its obligations in the short term, the future well-being of the company may never be achieved. Because the focus is on short-term items, current assets and current liabilities become most important.

To cover the entire scope of necessary information, the analyst must also consider long-term items. **Solvency** describes a company's ability to meet long-term debt obligations. Since the coverage is achieved through profitable operations, the income earned by the company must be utilized in conjunction with long-term items.

LO 2: Calculate financial ratios designed to measure a company's profitability, liquidity, and solvency.

Each of the areas, while important by itself, must be examined in conjunction with the others. Taken together, the ratios provide good insight into the financial management of the company. First, of course, the ratios must be applied to the information from a given firm. The **profitability ratios** incorporate measures of sales and net income, sometimes in conjunction with aspects of the balance sheet, to measure relationships of income generation. First, the **return on assets** divides the net income before taxes (the return) by total assets. This computation yields a percentage earned on the assets employed in the company. The **profit margin before income tax ratio** indicates the percentage of sales, before taxes are subtracted, that was earned. Net income before taxes is divided by sales to get a percentage profit margin before taxes. A very similar calculation is the **profit margin after tax ratio** which measures the percentage profit margin after taxes. The formula for this ratio is net income after taxes divided by sales. An additional measure of asset utilization can be found by dividing sales by total assets. This measure, called the **total asset turnover ratio** shows how effectively the company has used its total assets. The last two formulas are **return on equity after income taxes ratio** and the **return on equity before income taxes ratio**. The first formula divides net income after taxes by stockholders' equity while the second takes net income plus taxes and divides by stockholders' equity. These calculations indicate the percentage return enjoyed by equity holders during the period.

Liquidity calculations look to short-term items. The first, the **current ratio**, divides current assets by current liabilities. This often-used calculation tells the analyst the number of times current assets could be used to pay off current liabilities. A general assessment of the desirable number is two to one, but the nature of the business may make other relationships acceptable. A very stringent measure of short-term debt paying ability is the **quick ratio (also called acid-test ratio)**. The total of cash plus accounts receivable plus trading securities is divided by current liabilities. Essentially this formula measures the ease with which debts could be paid in a very short period; as a result, the relationship is generally closer to a one-to-one ratio. The **net sales to working capital ratio** divides sales by the difference between current assets and current liabilities. Working capital measures current assets in excess of current liabilities, so this formula evaluates the amount of sales being generated by this liquidity ratio. The last two ratios examine usage of individual current assets in generating positive outcomes for the company. The **receivables turnover ratio** divides net credit sales by accounts receivable. The measure tells the analyst how many times the company collected all of its receivables during the accounting period. The **average collection period**, the average number of days needed for the company to collect receivables, can be found by dividing the days in a year by the receivables turnover ratio. Similarly, the **inventory turnover ratio** divides cost of sales by inventory to get the number of times the company sold its inventory. Also, the number of days in a year divided by the inventory turnover ratio shows the average number of days a company holds its inventory before sale.

The third area of importance is **solvency**. These formulas examine how easily the company can meet its long-term debt obligations. The **debt ratio** measures the portion of assets financed by debt. Total liabilities divided by total assets indicates the percentage of assets on which debt is owed. The remainder of the assets have been financed by equity. The difference between debt and equity financing relates to the fact that interest must be paid on debt and the debt must be repaid as well. Equity financing does not carry such requirements. Last, the **coverage ratio** measures the number of times interest could be paid from earnings. Earnings before interest expense and income taxes is divided by interest expense to get a number of times the company could pay interest. A company that bears a large debt burden will find that the number of times it can pay interest will be much lower than a company that is financed more conservatively.

| LO 3: Locate industry averages. | Stand-alone ratios, while certainly of interest, provide far less meaningful information than those ratios compared |

with the outcomes which are normal for the industry in which the company operates. Industry information can be found in a variety of sources including the *Almanac of Business and Industrial Financial Ratios, RMA Annual Statement Studies* or *Industry Norms & Key Business Ratios*. An examination of a given company's ratio compared with industry averages provides a direct comparison of the quality of a given company's management with that of the competitors.

| LO 4: Evaluate a company's ratios using a comparison to industry | The first step in analyzing a company is to compare its ratios to the industry averages. Both **total industry amounts and the amounts for comparably-sized** |

firms should be observed. Sometimes the size of the company can make a big difference in the analyses. Therefore, both measures need to be gathered for the evaluation.

| LO 5: Use ratio values from consecutive time periods to evaluate the profitability, liquidity, and solvency of a business. | Results of a firm at a single point in time provide insights when compared with comparable companies in the same industry. An additional aid in analysis is to **examine the ratios of the company over time**. This |

procedure yields a type of trend analysis of the ratios and allows the analyst to reach conclusions about the growth or contraction of the company. Looking at the results over time can assist the analyst in identifying problem areas and areas which will separate a given company from others in the industry. While this separation may be bad or good, discovery of the trend early allows the analyst to make decisions about the company before, perhaps, others have seen what is happening.

| LO 6: Draw conclusions about the creditworthiness and investment- | Decisions based on the analyses just completed must be considered in the light of their being based on historical information. These analyses are, however, the best |

indicators anyone can have about the future. The trends, especially, can often be expected to continue. Utilizing the materials generated, then, the analyst makes decisions about whether the company is worthy of receiving loans or if it comprises an investment that should be made. Much of the ability to make such decisions comes with experience, but even novice analysts can make better decisions after these analyses than the decisions that could have been made without such examinations. The decision constitutes the outcome of the analysis which has been made. This decision, however, must be tempered by the problems inherent in the techniques we have used.

LO 7: State the limitations of ratio analysis.

Though ratio analysis is helpful, the analyst must recognize the important limitations of the technique. **First, the predictive value of the information depends greatly on the quality of the past information used.** The old idea of garbage-in, garbage-out is universally true. **A second issue lies in the fact that we are trying to obtain a hint of future information by using historical information.** In an era of rapidly changing conditions, historical data may not provide us with a good view of what we can expect in the future. **A third issue derives from the fact that year-end balance sheet numbers have been used.** Year-end numbers may differ significantly from the numbers experience by the company throughout the year. Fiscal years often end during the slowest times for companies, and balance sheet amounts may not be representative of year-long balances. Additionally, different accounting methods may create important differences between companies even though the companies themselves may be alike. **The last issue relates to lack of uniformity of specific ratio calculations.** Differences in basic formulas will, of course, make comparisons far less reliable than would exactness in the formulas.

CHAPTER GLOSSARY

Acid-test ratio: a stringent test of liquidity that compares highly liquid current assets to current liabilities. Also called the quick ratio

Coverage ratio: a ratio that indicates a company's ability to make its periodic interest payments. Also called the times interest earned ratio

Current ratio: a ratio that measures a company's ability to meet its current liabilities with cash generated from current assets

Debt ratio: a ratio that measures what proportion of a company's assets is financed by debt

Financial statement analysis: the process of looking beyond the face of the financial statements to gain additional insight into a company's financial health

Inventory turnover ratio: a ratio that indicates the number of times total merchandise inventory is purchased (or finished goods inventory is produced) and sold during a period

Liquidity: the ease with which an asset can be converted to cash

Liquidity ratios: ratios that evaluate a company's ability to generate sufficient cash to meet its short-term obligations

Net sales to working capital ratio: a ratio that indicates the level of sales generated for a given level of working capital

Profit margin before income tax ratio: a ratio that measures the profitability of sales before income taxes

Profit margin after income tax ratio: a ratio that measures the after-tax net income each sales dollar generates

Profitability: the ease with which a company generates income

Profitability ratios: ratios that measure a firm's past performance and help predict its future profitability level

Quick ratio: a stringent test of liquidity that compares highly liquid current assets to current liabilities. Also called the acid-test ratio

Ratio analysis: a technique for analyzing the relationship between two items from a company's financial statements for a given period

Receivables turnover ratio: a ratio that measures the liquidity of accounts receivable

Return on assets ratio: a ratio that measures how efficiently a company uses its assets to produce profits. Also called return on total assets

Return on equity after taxes ratio: a ratio that indicates how much after-tax income was generated for a given level of equity

Return on equity before taxes ratio: a ratio that calculates how much before-tax income was generated for a given level of equity

Return on total assets: a ratio that measures how efficiently a company uses its assets to produce profits. Also called return on assets ratio

Solvency: a company's ability to meet the obligations created by its long-term debt

Times interest earned ratio: a ratio that indicates a company's ability to make its periodic interest payments. Also called coverage ratio

Total asset turnover ratio: a ratio that calculates the amount of sales produced for a given level of assets used

Working capital: the difference between current assets and current liabilities

Analyzing Financial Statements for Profitability, Liquidity, and Solvency

PROBLEM APPLICATIONS

Multiple Choice Questions:

Multiple Choice Questions: For each of the following multiple choice questions, circle
the best response.

1. Harman Company had the following financial information available:

	2002	**2001**	**2000**
Revenues	184,794	179,410	174,184
Expenses	67,420	66,098	63,554
Net Income	117,374	113,312	110,630
Total assets	148,448	140,768	131,904
Total liabilities	70,906	68,178	64,930
Owners' equity	77,542	72,590	66,974

Based on this information, the trend of the company's debt ratio is:

A. getting better.
B. getting worse.
C. remaining static.
D. becoming volatile.

2. Below are the comparative current ratios of two companies:

	2002	**2001**	**2000**
Betty's Lanscaping, Inc.	1.64	1.25	1.20
Dirt Cheap Landscaping, Inc.	1.75	1.80	1.92

Based on this information

A. Betty's current liquidity is better than Dirt Cheap's, but is declining.
B. Betty's current liquidity is worse than Dirt Cheap's, but is improving.
C. Dirt Cheap's current liquidity is better than Betty's and is improving.
D. Dirt Cheap's current liquidity is worse than Betty's and is declining.

3. What are the broad categories of financial statement ratios?
A. Operating, investing, and financing
B. Liquidity, profitability, and solvency
C. Current ratio, price-earnings ratio, and debt to total assets ratio
D. Income statement ratio, balance sheet ratio, and statement of retained earnings
ratio

130

4. Which of the following ratios would give the best indication of a company's ability to meet its short-term obligations?
   A. Quick ratio
   B. Net sales to working capital ratio
   C. Receivables turnover ratio
   D. Debt ratio

5. Solvency ratios measure a company's
   A. short-term ability to pay its current obligations
   B. short-term ability to meet unexpected cash needs
   C. operating success for a given period of time
   D. ability to meet the obligations created by its long-term debt.

6. Which of the following statements regarding financial ratios is correct?
   A. The debt ratio and the current ratio are both measures of solvency.
   B. The current ratio and the profit margin after income tax ratio are both measures of liquidity.
   C. The return on assets ratio and total asset turnover ratio are both measures of profitability.
   D. The return on equity after income taxes ratio and the coverage ratio are both measures of solvency.

7. The information below relates to Wiggum, Inc.

Revenue	66,000
Wage expense	10,000
Total Liabilities	18,000
Cost of Goods Sold	31,000
Total Stockholder's Equity	29,000
Tax expense	6,000

Rounded to the nearest 1/10 of a percent, what is the company's return on assets?

   A. 40.4%
   B. 53.2%
   C. 86.2%
   D. 140.4%

8. Below are the coverage ratios of two companies:

Company A	Company B
15.25	12.50

Given this information

A. Company A is more likely to be able to make its periodic interest payments than Company B

B. Company B is more likely to be able to make its periodic interest payments than Company A

C. Company A must have a greater interest expense than Company B

D. Company B must have a greater interest expense than Company A

9. Assuming stable business conditions, an increase in the receivables turnover would probably indicate

A   credit monitoring is being neglected.

B   more customers are requesting credit.

C. payments are coming in more quickly.

D. more high-dollar items are being sold.

10. A downturn in the economy is often observable in a company's financial results as a

A. increase in the debt ratio.

B. increase in asset turnover.

C. increase in the coverage ratio.

D. increase in the current ratio.

11. If a company has a current ratio 1.5 to 1, the effect of paying off a long-term note payable would be

A. to increase the current ratio.

B. to decrease the current ratio.

C. to not affect the current ratio.

D. different than if the ratio were .5 to 1.

12. Which of the following can be used to evaluate long-term solvency?

A. Debt ratio.

B. Receivables turnover.

C. Return on assets.

D. Quick ratio.

True / False Questions:

1. Profitability ratios measure a firm's past performance and help predict its future profitability level.

2. Liquidity describes a company's ability to meet the obligations created by its long-term debt.

3. Return on assets ratio measures how efficiently the company uses its assets to produce profits.
4. Total asset turnover ratio is calculated as net income divided by total assets.
5. The receivable turnover ratio can be converted to the average collection period in days by dividing 365 days in the year by the receivables turnover.
6. The current ratio is a more stringent test of liquidity than the quick ratio.
7. The net-sales-to-working-capital ratio indicates the level of sales generated for a given level of working capital.
8. The debt ratio is calculated by dividing total liabilities by total assets.
9. The coverage ratio indicates a company's ability to make its periodic principal payments on debt.
10. Ratio analysis should include a review of the company's ratios over a multi-year period to identify possible trends.
11. Comparing ratios across time or with other companies is generally not cost-effective.
12. A problem with industry comparisons is the diversity of many companies.

Matching Questions :

_____ 1. Receivable turnover ratio

_____ 2. Return on equity after taxes ratio

_____ 3. Net sales to working capital ratio

_____ 4. Total asset turnover ratio

_____ 5. Inventory turnover ratio

_____ 6. Current ratio

_____ 7. Profit margin after income tax ratio

_____ 8. Debt ratio

_____ 9. Return on assets ratio

_____ 10. Coverage ratio

A. Measures how efficiently the company uses its assets to produce profits.
B. Indicates the level of sales generated for a given level of working capital.
C. Indicates a company's ability to make its periodic interest payments.
D. Indicates how much after-tax income was generated for a given level of equity.
E. Calculates the amount of sales produced for a given level of assets used.
F. Measures how quickly a company collects its accounts receivable.
G. Indicates the number of times total merchandise inventory is purchased and sold during a period.
H. Measures the amount of after-tax net income generated by a dollar of sales.
I. Measures the proportion of assets financed by debt.
J. Indicates a company's ability to meet short-term obligations.

Analyzing Financial Statements for Profitability, Liquidity, and Solvency

Exercises:

1. Below are partial comparative balance sheets for the Carlson Company:

	2003	2002	2001
Assets			
Cash	884,670	1,251,532	446,131
Accounts Receivable	775,339	726,541	585,761
Inventory	1,409,736	1,633,327	1,757,664
Other Current Assets	33,165	41,311	57,623
Total Current Assets	3,102,910	3,652,711	2,847,179
Liabilities			
Accounts Payable	1,278,659	1,529,017	1,158,011
Short Term Debt	1,410	112,310	133,588
Total Current Liabilities	1,280,069	1,641,327	1,291,599

Calculate the company's current ratio for the years available and evaluate the trend.

2. Below is a trend of the return on equity after taxes ratio for the Royal Company:

	2003	2002	2001
Return on equity after taxes	8.5%	7.6%	7.2%

Evaluate the trend and speculate on possible causes of the trend.

3. Below is a trend of the debt ratio and coverage ratio for the Tenenbaum Company:

	2003	2002	2001
Debt ratio	38.8%	36.0%	35.4%
Coverage ratio	16.2	18.4	20.6

Evaluate the solvency trend and speculate on possible causes of the trend.

4. Below are several liquidity trends for the Paltrow Company:

	2003	2002	2001
Current ratio	2.54	2.30	2.22
Quick ratio	1.62	1.77	1.84
Receivable turnover ratio	12.50	14.60	15.80
Inventory turnover ratio	26.30	24.10	23.30

Evaluate the company's liquidity and draw conclusions regarding the trend.

5. Review the information and your results to Exercises #1-4 and discuss any limitations to the use of ratio analysis.

Problems:

1.   The comparative financial statements of Hobson, Inc. and Williams Company are below.

	Hobson, Inc.			Williams Company		
	2003	**2002**	**2001**	**2003**	**2002**	**2001**
Revenue	2,006,078	1,621,886	1,214,100	1,853,629	1,427,339	953,067
Cost of Goods Sold	330,132	268,386	235,264	279,637	202,391	162,881
Gross Profit	1,675,946	1,353,500	978,836	1,573,992	1,224,948	790,186
Less Expenses						
Selling and General	977,494	766,382	525,450	588,083	495,068	338,794
Research and Development	145,216	138,069	104,636	31,061	21,851	21,186
Interest	1,913	1,623	1,153	2,348	1,611	1,456
Taxes	66,757	57,746	55,475	99,447	69,147	64,394
Net Income	484,566	389,680	292,122	853,053	637,271	364,356
Assets						
Cash	203,551	140,524	109,645	494,912	461,011	310,972
Accounts Receivable	297,673	226,092	167,648	198,641	162,758	113,612
Inventory	114,667	108,507	96,988	72,220	49,946	26,320
Other Current Assets	86,906	82,425	62,312	109,062	85,470	82,216
Total Current Assets	702,797	557,548	436,593	874,835	759,185	533,120
Property and Equipment, net	840,330	875,656	1,278,530	1,689,147	1,213,859	1,124,568
Total Assets	1,543,127	1,433,204	1,715,123	2,563,982	1,973,044	1,657,688
Liabilities						
Accounts Payable	218,147	213,083	205,560	279,729	290,804	276,313
Short Term Debt	5,182	3,617	2,970	215,908	149,834	135,501
Total Current Liabilities	223,329	216,700	208,530	495,637	440,638	411,814
Long Term Liabilities	22,718	20,295	13,798	660,711	607,355	613,640
Equity						
Common Stock	384	384	384	974	801	611
Additional Paid-In Capital	3,974	3,974	3,974	13,300	10,348	7,493
Retained Earnings	1,292,722	1,191,851	1,488,437	1,393,360	913,902	624,130
Total Liabilities & Equity	1,543,127	1,433,204	1,715,123	2,563,982	1,973,044	1,657,688

1.   Calculate the following ratios for the years available for each company:

Coverage ratio
Current ratio
Debt ratio
Inventory turnover
Profit margin after income tax ratio
Receivable turnover ratio
Return on assets ratio

2.   Assess each company's relative liquidity, profitability and solvency.

SOLUTIONS

Multiple Choice Questions:

1. A	7. B
2. B	8. A
3. B	9. C
4. A	10. A
5. D	11. B
6. C	12. A

True / False Questions:

1. True
2. False; liquidity describes the ease with which an asset can be converted to cash. Solvency is a company's ability to meet the obligations created by its long-term debt.
3. True
4. False; total asset turnover ratio is calculated as sales divided by total assets.
5. True
6. False; the quick ratio is a more stringent test of liquidity than the current ratio.
7. True
8. True
9. False; the coverage ratio indicates a company's ability to make its periodic interest payments.
10. True
11. False; the data are fairly quick to generate and provides much improved information.
12. True

Matching Solutions
1.   F
2.   D

3.   B
4.   E
5.   G
6.   J
7.   H
8.   I
9.   A
10.   C

Exercises:

1.

Year	Current Ratio	
2003	2.42	(3,102,910 / 1,280,069)
2002	2.23	(3,652,711 / 1,641,327)
2001	2.20	(2,847,179 / 1,291,599)

The company's current ratio is improving each year. From 2001 to 2002, current assets grew at a faster rate than current liabilities and from 2002 to 2003, although current assets decreased, current liabilities had a more significant decrease.

2. A company's return on equity after taxes ratio indicates how much after-tax income was generated for a given level of equity. In this case, the company's ratio is improving each year. This was most likely caused by an increase in net income each period along with either stable overall equity or a decrease in equity through dividend or treasury share transactions. The increase in net income could be the result of higher sales or lower cost of goods sold, administrative or tax expenses or some related combination.

3. A company's debt ratio measures what proportion of a company's assets is financed by debt and its coverage ratio indicates a company's ability to make its periodic interest payments. The company's solvency appears to be declining because its debt ratio is increasing each year indicating that the company has more debt relative to its assets while its coverage ratio is declining which indicates that the company is less able to make periodic payments related to the debt.

4. The company's overall liquidity is improving as seen in the increase in the current ratio; however, the quick ratio, a more stringent test of liquidity is declining. The company has been less effective at collecting receivables, and the company's inventory appears to be selling more quickly as evidenced by the increase in the inventory turnover ratio.

5. First, attempting to predict the future using past results depends upon the predictive value of the information we use. Second, the financial statements used to compute the ratios are based on historical cost. Third, figures from the balance sheet used to

calculate the ratios are year-end numbers which may not be representative of the rest of the year. Fourth, industry peculiarities create difficulty in comparing the ratios of a company in one industry with those of a company in another industry. Fifth, lack of uniformity concerning what is to be included in the numerators and denominators of specific ratios makes comparison to published industry averages extremely difficult. Perhaps the greatest single limitation of ratio analysis is that people tend to place too much reliance on the ratios. Ratio analysis only enriches all the other information decision makers should consider when making credit, investment, and similar types of decisions.

Problem:

	Hobson, Inc.			Williams Company		
	2003	**2002**	**2001**	**2003**	**2002**	**2001**
Profitability						
Profit margin after income tax ratio	24.15%	24.03%	24.06%	46.02%	44.65%	38.23%
Return on assets ratio	35.73%	31.22%	20.27%	37.15%	35.80%	25.86%
Liquidity						
Current ratio	3.15	2.57	2.09	1.77	1.72	1.29
Receivable turnover ratio	6.74	7.17	7.24	9.33	8.77	8.39
Inventory turnover	2.88	2.47	2.43	3.87	4.05	6.19
Solvency						
Coverage ratio	289.20	276.68	302.47	406.66	439.50	295.47
Debt ratio	15.94%	16.54%	12.96%	45.10%	53.12%	61.86%

Hobson's profit margin after income tax ratio appears fairly stable; however, the company's return on assets has generally improved indicating that the company is using its assets more productively. Williams is more efficient in its use of assets as compared to Hobson which is reflected in the company's higher profit margin after income tax.

Hobson's overall liquidity seems to be better than Williams; however, the overall liquidity of both companies is improving based on their respective current ratios. The trend for Hobson's receivable turnover should be a concern for the company as it is continually declining; whereas, Williams' inventory turnover should also be addressed by management given its downward trend.

Williams appears to rely much more on debt than Hobson based on its debt ratio; however, this may not be problematic as its ability to cover periodic interest payments is much better.

Chapter 9
Using Relevant Information
for Internal Operations

CHAPTER SUMMARY

Various analytical tools help in making internal decisions in an objective manner. These decisions may be special types, or they may be fairly ordinary and regular decisions. To the extent possible, however, they should be made objectively. Eliminating human biases helps the manager to see what "just the numbers" say about the decision. Of course, the human aspects of decision-making are important, but the numbers should be the starting point.

LO 1: Determine the fixed and variable components of a cost element using the high-low method and results of regression analysis.

Since fixed costs behave in a distinctly different manner than do variable costs, one of the most important steps in a business requires that fixed and variable costs be separated. **One method of accomplishing this task is through application of high-low analysis.** The total cost formula given earlier in the text states that total cost equals fixed cost plus the unit variable cost times some level of activity. The high-low method utilizes the idea that measures at the highest and lowest levels of activity will yield measures of fixed and variable costs.

To determine costs to fit into the total cost formula, the analyst should identify the highest and lowest level of activity within a data set. Using these two points as activity bounds, the costs at those levels are utilized. The difference in the two activity levels and the difference in the two cost amounts are computed. The difference in cost is then divided by the difference in activity level to determine the variable cost per unit of activity. When the variable cost is known, the total cost formula is then utilized to determine fixed costs. Either level of activity can be employed to determine fixed costs, but the analyst must use care to align the total cost and activity level. When both fixed and variable costs have been computed, the formula should be rewritten as the total cost equal to the computed fixed cost plus the computed variable cost times an activity level.

Although **regression analysis** appears in the appendix to this chapter, we shall discuss it here since it provides an alternative and more precise method of separating fixed and variable costs. Use of the regression analysis requires some knowledge of the way costs are graphed. To present total costs in graphic format, the analyst uses the vertical axis (y axis) to show costs and the horizontal axis (x) to show activity. The point at which a total cost line intersects the vertical axis indicates the total fixed cost while the slope of the line (the amount of rise in the line for each additional unit of activity) comprises the variable cost per unit. A regression program in a spreadsheet or on a mainframe program will utilize all observations and compute a line which fits the data most closely (so that the squared differences between each observation and the line are the smallest total number that can be found). The program will then provide output indicating the value of the intercept of the line (the fixed costs) and the x variable measuring the slope of the line (the variable cost). Regression provides the most precise analysis since it uses data from all observations rather than from just the two extreme activity points.

LO 2: Identify the characteristics of a relevant cost or revenue.

Given time constraints on managers and other analysts of information, an ability to select only those **items which are relevant to a given decision is vital in terms of saving time and money.** In general, those costs which have already been incurred are not relevant since, no matter what decision a manager makes, those past costs, called **sunk costs, cannot be changed**. They must, therefore, be ignored. Also **irrelevant are those costs which do not differ between the alternatives being considered.** While they must be paid, the alternative selected will make no difference—they will have to be paid regardless of the alternative selected. Some practice is often needed to develop an understanding of the costs that are relevant and those that are not.

LO 3: Demonstrate why sunk costs and costs that do not differ between alternatives are irrelevant costs.

Sunk costs are those that have already been incurred. No matter how much we might want to do so, we cannot go back and undo a past decision. Neither can we get back money which has already been spent. Since the "undo" part is not available to us, sunk costs must be ignored. In much the same manner, **if a cost is the same regardless of which alternative we take, it really cannot impact our decision.** We are, unfortunately, somewhat helpless at altering items which are the same no matter what we do. Thus, neither sunk costs, which cannot be undone, and non-differential costs, which are the same no matter what we do, should both be ignored in our decision-making. They contribute no information but do take up space and clutter the analysis.

LO 4: Discuss several major qualitative factors that should be considered when making a business decision.

Relevant costs are among the easiest parts of a decision since these are quantifiable. We can put numbers to them and measure them in money. At the same time, other factors must be considered which are much more difficult to evaluate. **In addition to monetary factors, managers must be sensitive to such items as employee morale, quality of product, customer satisfaction, customer perception, community perception, and so forth.** Sometimes managers find that the qualitative factors outweigh the quantitative factors even though the quantitative factors may have indicated that a specific decision should be made. No manager can afford to stop the analysis once relevant revenues and costs have been identified.

LO 5: Use accounting information to determine the relevant cost of various decisions.

Certain costs consistently impact selected business decisions. For example, the **equipment replacement** decision generally must include the cost of the new equipment while costs related to purchase and past use

140

of the old equipment are irrelevant, since they are past. Differential future labor and maintenance costs on the two pieces of equipment are relevant, but past costs again should not be considered. Additionally, the residual values of the two machines are relevant. An final consideration that needs to be incorporated regards the differences in cash flows over time. When the relevant costs have been identified, the manager has the information necessary to make the decision. The impact of including the adjustments for the time value of money will be incorporated in a later chapter.

Another common decision relates to the opportunity to take a special order. **Special orders are those occasional opportunities to provide large amounts of product on a one-time basis to a customer.** These orders may require special labeling, or they may include a request for a price reduction. A critical component of this decision lies in whether the supplier has already covered fixed costs in regular production and has the ability to meet the request without upsetting regular production and losing regular sales. If regular production and sales can be continued, the only relevant costs are variable; in such a case, any inflow above variable costs will contribute to profit for the company.

Make-or-buy decisions relate to the outsourcing decision. Should a company make a product or provide a service within its own facilities, or should it contract with a vendor outside the company? Generally, the relevant costs of this decision are the variable expenses that can be avoided as compared with the outside cost. Fixed costs are not relevant because these will continue no matter what decision is made. Alternative uses of fixed cost items may, however, become available and then must be considered.

Decisions to expand or contract the size of the business often occur in changing economic times. Whether the business should undertake this fairly significant step occur because the company has too much activity to be supported by current facilities or the company has idle capacity. The **decision to add or close divisions** constitutes one of the more significant decisions because the cost often becomes very high. Decisions to expand depend on the ability of the company to produce an extra item which can be sold at a price which exceeds the variable costs of the product. Any amount by which the product's selling price exceeds variable costs usually provides incentive to continue it as long as fixed costs do not increase. When multiple products are involved, the products with the highest contribution margin should be the ones to be continued.

LO 6: Interpret the effects of fixed costs and opportunity costs on various decisions.

The impact of fixed costs and opportunity costs tends to be relatively constant in decision-making. **Fixed costs occur in fairly large monetary blocks and must be considered in total.** They cannot be easily changed, and once incurred are with the company for a long period of time. Decisions regarding fixed costs already incurred generally tend toward making the maximum use of the already-incurred costs. **Opportunity costs relate to foregone inflows.** Making a decision to go to school, for example, often means giving up income from a job. In other words, the decision cost included not getting something that had been received in the past or which could be received with a different decision. While the concept seems a bit awkward, people automatically include, in everyday decisions, the effects of opportunities that must be given up in order to pursue another path.

CHAPTER GLOSSARY

High-low method: a model that separates the fixed and variable components of a cost element by using the mathematical differences between the highest and lowest levels of activity within a relevant range

Opportunity cost: the value of what is relinquished because of choosing one alternative over another

Outsourcing: buying services, products, or components of products from outside vendors instead of producing them

Qualitative factors: non-numerical attributes that affect decision alternatives

Quantitative factors: factors that affect business decisions and are represented by numbers

Regression analysis: a mathematical model that uses all the items in the data set to compute a least squares regression line that equals the total cost formula

Relevant cost: a future cost that is pertinent to a particular decision and differs between two decision alternatives of production volume

Relevant costing: the process of determining which dollar inflows and outflows pertain to a particular management decision

Relevant revenue: a future revenue that differs between two decision alternatives

Special order: an order that is outside a business's normal scope of business activity

Sunk costs: past expenditures that current or future actions cannot change

Time value of money: the interest-earning potential of cash over time

PROBLEM APPLICATIONS

Multiple Choice Questions: For each of the following multiple choice questions, circle the letter of the BEST response.

1. The Ace Company had the following information available:

	2003	2002	2001	2000
Units produced	1,200	1,150	1,350	800
Total cost of production	23,000	22,250	25,250	17,000

Using the high-low method, what is the company's fixed cost?

   A. 5,000
   B. 12,000
   C. 17,000
   D. 18,000

2. The following information is available for Pinnacle, Incorporated:

Period	Number of Units Produced	Total Cost of Production
Month 1	150,000	545,500
Month 2	163,000	582,810
Month 3	172,000	608,640

Using the high-low method, what is the company's variable cost per unit?
   A. $0.77
   B. $2.67
   C. $2.77
   D. $2.87

3. The high-low method
   A. determines fixed cost first.
   B. gives an exact measure of costs.
   C. uses all data.
   D. depends on the total cost formula.

4. Qualitative factors are
   A. numerical factors that affect business decisions.
   B. future costs that are pertinent to a particular decision and differ between decision alternatives.
   C. non-numerical attributes that affect decision alternatives.
   D. costs that cannot be changed by current and future actions.

5.   What considerations can be ignored for a special order
      A.   Plant capacity
      B.   Fixed costs
      C.   Variable costs
      D.   Sales price

6.   Sunk costs
      A.   should be ignored.
      B.   are pertinent to a particular decision.
      C.   are considered a qualitative factor
      D.   should only be considered in a special order decision

7.   ˙ When making decisions managers should rely on
      A.   relevant quantitative factors, but at least consider qualitative factors.
      B.   relevant qualitative factors, but at least consider quantitative factors.
      C.   relevant qualitative factors only
      D.   relevant quantitative factors only

8.   Opportunity costs
      A.   are not real.
      B.   can be qualitative.
      C.   should not be considered.
      D.   often require high payouts.

9.   Any cost which bears on a particular decision is a/an
      A.   sunk cost.
      B.   reliable cost.
      C.   relevant cost.
      D.   opportunity cost.

10.   In a decision to replace an old machine, a manager must always consider the
      A.   cost of the new machine.
      B.   depreciation taken on the old machine.
      C.   image of new factory equipment.
      D.   lost productivity of selling the old machine.

11.   An outsourcing decision requires consideration of
      A.   jobs lost.
      B.   revenues produced.
      C.   continued training in-house to maintain skills.
      D.   comparative costs.

12. Regression analysis is better than high-low analysis because
    A. it is easier.
    B. it uses all data.
    C. more people understand it.
    D. it gives exact measures of cost behavior.

True / False Questions:

1. A relevant cost is any cost that relates to a particular decision.
2. Sunk costs are past costs that cannot be changed by current or future actions.
3. Outsourcing is buying services, products or components of products from outside vendors instead of producing them.
4. A special order is an order that is outside a company's normal scope of business activity.
5. Qualitative factors are factors that affect business decisions which are based on numbers while quantitative factors are non-numerical attributes that affect decision alternatives.
6. Common business decisions include whether or not to replace equipment, whether a company should accept a special order, whether to outsource as well as whether to add or close divisions.
7. Fixed costs normally are relevant in make-or-buy decisions.
8. Opportunity costs are all of the costs that are relevant to a particular decision.
9. Only two points of activity are needed for the high-low method of cost analysis.
10. Regression analysis is more complicated to perform that the high-low method.
11. Depreciation is irrelevant in equipment replacement decisions.
12. Future costs can never be called sunk costs.

Matching:

1. Match each numbered item with the letter of its definition.

_____	1 quantitative factors	_____ 6 special order
_____	2 sunk cost	_____ 7 qualitative factors
_____	3 Outsourcing	_____ 8 relevant cost
_____	4 relevant revenue	_____ 9 high-low method
_____	5 regression analysis	_____ 10 opportunity cost

A   an order that is outside its normal scope of business activity.

B   non-numerical attributes that affect decision alternatives.

C   is the value of what is given up because of choosing one alternative over another.

D   is a model that separates the fixed and variable components of a cost element by using the mathematical differences between the highest and lowest levels of activity within a relevant range of production volume.

E   buying services, products or components of products from outside vendors instead of producing them.

F   factors that affect business decisions which are based on numbers.

G   a mathematical model that uses all the items in the data set to compute a least squares regression line that equals the total cost formula.

H   A future revenue that differs between two decision alternatives

I   is a future cost that is pertinent to a particular decision and differs between decision alternatives.

J   a cost that cannot be changed by current or future actions.

2. Identify each of the following costs as relevant (R) or irrelevant (I) for the decision specified.

Replacement decision:

_____ 1. Cost of the old machine
_____ 2. Cost of the new machine
_____ 3. Wages of the machine operator
_____ 4. Cost of operating the new machine.
_____ 5. Color of the machine

Make-or-buy decision:

_____ 1. Costs currently being spent for production of item
_____ 2. Idle space caused by outsourcing decision
_____ 3. Dependability of supplier
_____ 4. Cost of unemployment for laid-off employees
_____ 5. Cost of item being purchased from outside vendor

Special order decision:

_____ 1. Revenue from subletting idle space
_____ 2. Allocated fixed costs
_____ 3. Cost of special logo for customer
_____ 4. Overtime wages to meet early deadline
_____ 5. Maintenance on machines

Exercises:

1. The following information is for the Mission Company

	2003	**2002**
Units Produced	296,000	187,000
Total Manufacturing Costs	5,660,000	3,589,000

    Use the high-low method to determine the variable cost element and fixed cost component for the company. Write the total cost formula using the numbers you've computed.

2. Don Pitzer is considering buying a new automobile; list five or more quantitative and five or more qualitative factors he should consider.

3. The Arrow Company is considering purchasing new office equipment. To help make the decision the company is planning to send an employee to a trade show sponsored by the various equipment manufacturers. List five or more relevant factors the company should consider regarding the equipment in addition to sending the employee to the trade show.

4. Maverick Hi-Fi manufactures custom home stereo products and is considering buying a particular type of circuit board it uses in its products. The company has the current manufacturing costs for 10,000 units related to the circuit board as follow:

Direct material	$1.50	per unit
Direct labor	$2.75	per unit
Variable overhead	$2.25	per unit
Fixed overhead	$1.20	total

The fixed overhead could not be avoided if the company stopped making the circuit board. The supplier will sell Maverick the component for $7.00 per unit.

a. Should Maverick continue making the component or purchase it from the supplier?

b. Now assume that the supplier is willing to sell the component to Maverick for $6.00 per unit. Should Maverick continue making the component or purchase it from the supplier?

c. Assume, instead, that, in addition to the offer from a supplier to provide the component at $6.00, Maverick has received an offer from another manufacturer to rent its manufacturing space for $12,500. Should Maverick continue to make the component or purchase it from the supplier?

d. List five or more qualitative factors that Maverick might want to consider in its decision.

5. Williams Enterprises uses a specialized computer to produce its invoices and is considering updating this computer with a newer, faster model. The current computer was purchased for $15,000, has annual operating costs of $5,000, and if sold now would have a salvage value of $2,000. If not sold now, the computer could be used for another five years but would then be worthless. The new computer could be purchased for $25,000, has expected operating costs of $3,000 and is expected to have a zero salvage value as the end of its five-year useful life. Should the current computer be replaced at this time?

Problems:

1.   The Simpson Company manufactures a line of high quality home furnishings including sofas, chairs and tables. The company's most popular line of sofas is the BeHi model which sells for $1,300 each. The company has been approached by MegaMart, a large discount retail chain, with a request that the Simpson produce a similar, but lower cost model, the BeLo, for its chain of stores. MegaMart is willing to pay Simpson $1,000 for each of the 1,000 sofas in their order. Simpson's manufacturing costs related to the sofa are below:

	Per Unit
Direct material	$300
Direct labor	$200
Variable overhead	$400
Fixed overhead	$100
Total	$1,000

Simpson has available capacity to produce the additional sofas without any decrease in current production. Determine the following for the supervisory in charge of making the decision to accept the offer or not:

a.   What would be the change in Simpson's net income if it accepts the special order?

b.   What are five or more qualitative factors Simpson should consider before accepting the special order?

2.   Joe, a university professor, has planned to take his family on a two-week Disney Land vacation for over a year now, and his five children are very excited. His wife has scheduled four weeks off from her job to get everything ready and to go. They plan to leave next week. Joe's department head now has called him in to announce that Joe has been given the wonderful opportunity to teach a special course for visiting officials—next week. The pay would be double Joe's regular pay, and the people he would meet can help the university get extra funding. No one else in the department could teach the course, and the date cannot be changed.

a.   What quantitative factors must Joe consider?

b.   What qualitative factors must Joe consider?

c.   How does this decision differ from the type discussed in your text?

SOLUTIONS

Multiple Choice Questions:

1.	A	7.	A
2.	D	8.	B
3.	D	9.	C
4.	C	10.	A
5.	B	11.	D
6.	A	12.	B

True / False Questions:

1. False; a relevant cost is a future cost that is pertinent to a particular decision and differs between decision alternatives.
2. True
3. True
4. True
5. False; quantitative factors are based on numbers; qualitative factors are not.
6. True
7. False; fixed costs are normally irrelevant in such decisions because they cannot easily be changed in the short run.
8. False: opportunity costs are the foregone inflows that result from a given decision.
9. True
10. True
11. True
12. True

Matching:

1.

1.	F	6.	A
2.	J	7.	B
3.	E	8.	I
4.	H	9.	D
5.	G	10.	C

2.

Replacement decision:

1.	I
2.	R
3.	R
4.	R
5.	I

Make-or-buy decision

1.	R
2.	I
3.	R
4.	R
5.	R

Special order decision:

1.	R
2.	I
3.	R
4.	R.
5.	R

Exercises:

1.

	Units Produced	**Mfg. Costs**
2003	296,000	$5,660,000
2004	187,000	3,589,000
Difference	109,000	$2,071,000

$$\frac{\text{Change in costs}}{\text{Change in activity}} \quad \frac{\$2,071,000}{109,000} \quad = \quad \$19 \text{ per unit}$$

Total cost = Fixed cost + Variable cost (activity level)
$3,589,000 = FC + $19 (187,000)
$3,589,000 = 36,000 + $3,553,000

OR

$5,660,000 = FC + $19 (296,000)
$5,660,000 = 36,000 + $5,624,000

2.   **Quantitative factors to be considered**:
      1.   Cost of new car
      2.   Trade-in value of old car
      3.   Cost of insurance
      4.   Gasoline mileage
      5.   Cost of financing
      6.   Taxes on new car
      7.   Cost of tag

      Qualitative factors to be considered:
      1.   The color he wants
      2.   New car smell
      3.   How good he will look in that new car
      4.   How impressed his friends will be
      5.   Extra time he will have to work to make payments

3.   **Quantitative factors to be considered:**
      1.   Cost of travel, food, and lodging
      2.   Cost of information collection
      3.   Maintenance costs of equipment
      4.   Cost of operating equipment
      5.   Cost of training personnel
      6.   Freight and setup costs

      Qualitative factors to be considered:
      1.   Employee pride in new equipment
      2.   Frustration of employees with learning new equipment
      3.   Upset of changing from old to new
      4.   Disagreements among employees as to items to purchase
      5.   Lack of backup if all systems are changed at once
      6.   Possibility of lost files and information

4a.   In the first scenario, the company should make the component. The cost to buy
      exceeds even the variable costs of continuing to make internally.

	Make	**Buy**
Direct material	1.50	
Direct labor	2.75	
Variable overhead	2.25	
Purchase price		7.00
	6.50	7.00

4b.   Now Maverick should continue to make the component if no other use can be
      found for the idle space. If Maverick outsources the parts, it will be incurring

$12,000 of fixed overhead with no way to recover it. The company will be worse off by $7,000 per period ($12,000 fixed overhead less $5,000 savings on parts).

4c.   With the additional information that Maverick can rent out the idle space for $500 more than its cost, the company would be better off to buy the parts from the other supplier and rent out the space. Total savings would be $5,500 (.50 per part times 10,000 plus $500 improvement in coverage of fixed overhead)

4d.   Qualitative factors to consider:
1.   Dependability of supplier
2.   Possibility of supplier increasing price
3.   Possibility of renter not renewing rental agreement
4.   Need to lay off employees and morale of other employees
5.   Lack of control over quality of parts
6.   Effects of increased or decreased need for parts

5.   The company should keep the old equipment based on a cost savings of $13,000, calculated as follows:

	Keep	**Replace**
Start-up Costs		(25,000)
Operating Costs*	(25,000)	(15,000)
Shut-down costs		2,000
	(25,000)	(38,000)

* current computer = $5,000 x 5 years = $25,000
  new computer = $3,000 x 5 years = $15,000

Problems:

1a.   Simpson would generate additional operating income of $100,000 calculated as:

	Per Unit
Revenue	1,000
Less Costs	
Direct material	300
Direct labor	200
Variable overhead	400
Operating Income	100
x 1,000 units =	100,000

1b.   **Qualitative factors:**

1.   Effect on reputation of being associated with lower-quality sofa
2.   Effect on current market if a lower-priced alternative is available.
3.   Potential problems in dealing with a discounter
4.   Possibility of increased demand by discounter
5.   Reaction of current dealers to the special deal

2 a.   **Quantitative factors:**

1.   Loss of wages for teaching special course
2.   Cost of vacation
3.   Loss of wife's wages
4.   Loss of future funding opportunities for the university

2b.   **Qualitative factors:**

1.   Wife's anger
2.   Children's anger—times 5
3.   Department head's anger
4.   University President's anger
5.   Vacation loss
6.   Professional opportunities
7.   Loss of ability to make contacts to help in future endeavors

2c. Unlike other questions you have addressed, this one deals with a more personal, less business-oriented decision. The qualitative factors seem more important as decisions become more personalized. This decision has been personalized. For employees and people impacted directly by business decisions, the most important factors are apt to be personalized and, therefore, more qualitative. The emphasis in business is more objective and tends more toward the quantitative factors.

Chapter 10
Internal Planning
and Measurement Tools

CHAPTER SUMMARY

As part of the operating process, companies must plan for the future in order for managers to gain perspective on the way the company will look in the next months, or even years. The monetary plans are called budgets and include several documents prepared together. The master budget, sometimes called the operating budget, pulls together many parts of the company so the financial impacts can be estimated and predicted. These budgets allow managers to gain some idea of the direction the company will take in the coming period and allow them to plan for potential problems.

> **LO 1:** Discuss some of the benefits of the operating budget.

Four benefits accrue to a company that budgets conscientiously. **First, the budget provides a guide for the company to follow.** Of course, the business must be flexible enough to adapt to changing conditions, but the budget can help direct activities.

A second benefit of the budget lies in its aid to the business in resource allocation. The budgeting process requires that managers address priorities for resource allocation and decide where resources should be utilized. Without the budget, resource decisions would have to be made without adequate discussion or planning.

Third, developing the budget requires managers to work together and, therefore, forces managers to communicate and coordinate efforts. This communication establishes a rapport among managers that aids them in other efforts in managing the business.

A fourth benefit of budgeting accrues from the establishment of performance standards. The budget requires setting realistic goals, and various segments of the business work to achieve those goals. Budgeted goals become benchmarks against which companies compare actual performance to determine differences from goals and to examine causes of the differences.

> **LO 2:** Compare and contrast various approaches to preparing and using the operating budget.

Logic would indicate that after a number of years of making and improving budgets, companies would have arrived at a model that works best. Such is not the case. Multiple approaches to budgeting are in use by various businesses and other entities, and each method has its virtues and drawbacks. The **perpetual budget**, for example, continually adds a month to the budget when a month has passed on the old budget. This constant extension of the process allows the company personnel to have a twelve-month perspective on company plans. The problem with this

157

approach lies in the tendency of personnel to begin to budget automatically without considering the decisions being made.

For many years, **incremental budgeting** was the budgeting method of choice. This approach simply takes the previous period's budget and adds some increment for growth. The primary problem inherent in incremental budgeting lies in the lack of examination of prior year's budgeted amounts. If the previous budget was too high in some areas, that waste was incrementally greater in the following budget(s). This budget does, however, "make sense" to most people and is, therefore, more acceptable to the general group.

As an attempt to curb built-in wastefulness, some organizations adopted **zero-based budgeting.** This method starts with zero every year, and all budgeted amounts must be justified. The biggest problem with this type of budget comes from the high time commitment of starting over each period.

Top-down budgeting starts at the high levels of an organization and flows downward. Such a process ignores input from lower-level managers and workers and generally requires less time to build. Top management knows more about the firm overall and need to consult fewer people in building the budget. Disadvantages of such budgeting evolve as less acceptance of the budget by lower-level managers and lack of knowledge of daily operations by upper-level management. Top-down budgeting tends to be an **imposed budget** on lower levels of management and workers. The lower levels simply receive the budget with no opportunity for them to have input or offer suggestions.

Bottom-up budgeting, however, works from lower levels of management to upper levels with upper level's input being review and coordination of departmental information. Several advantages accrue from such an approach. Budgeting may be **more realistic** since the people preparing the budget actually work directly with it. Also, the lower-level managers and workers are **more apt to work toward accomplishment** of their budget. And last, in the process of budget preparation, employees **gain perspective on the company as a whole** rather than just their own isolated department. This type of budgeting utilizes the **participative budget approach,** incorporating the efforts of employees from many levels in the organization. Such an approach **empowers the employees** by giving them more responsibility and input into the decisions involving their jobs.

LO 3: Construct the three budgeted financial statements

The **budgeted income statement, budgeted balance sheet, and budgeted cash flow statement** evolve from the numbers generated on the preceding statements prepared in the master budgeting process. These statements incorporate all of the information generated during the process in order that the managers of the company can have a good idea of how the financial statements will appear at the end of the accounting period. As the examination of the budgeting process progresses, keeping this outcome in mind will help in making sense of the process.

LO 4: Demonstrate the role of the sales forecast in the budgeting process.

The first item on a budgeted income statement is the sales figure. **And the first item, the starting point, for all budgeting is the sales projections.** All other activities depend on the amount of forecasted sales since all other activities of the company relate to working toward being able to accomplish sales projections.

LO 5: Prepare the budgets included in the operating budget.

Starting with the **sales budget**, which provides the revenue expectations for the company, the work toward accomplishing the sales target can be quantified. The sales budget provides the expected revenue, anticipated ending inventory, and expected cash inflows from sales. These numbers are used on the projected income statement, balance sheet, and statement of cash flows.

Of course, once the sales projections are quantified, the goal then becomes planning for having goods available to sell. For manufacturers, this need for goods to sell requires the construction of **the production budget.** Merchandisers must prepare a **purchases budget** to identify amounts to buy. From the information on product purchases and uses, the company can budget for **cost of sales or cost of services** for the period. These budgets also yield information on ending inventories, cost of goods, and expected cash disbursements to pay for purchased inventory items. All of these amounts provide information, again, for the income statement, balance sheet, and statement of cash flows.

Additionally, the company must continue to include costs to support these activities by having people to sell goods and manage the business. The next budget, then, would be the **selling and administrative expense budget.** This budget includes items which feed into the income statement, balance sheet, and statement of cash flows.

The **cash budget** shows inflows from sales as well as outflows for goods and services and selling and administrative expense. Additional cash flows may include such items as dividends received or paid, equipment purchases or sales, loan payments or borrowing, and other miscellaneous items. The ending cash budget balance shows the cash balance on the balance sheet.

A **budgeted income statement** uses sales projections from the sales budget, product costs from the cost of goods sold or cost of services budget, selling and administrative expense from the selling and administrative budget, and estimated tax to be paid on the anticipated profit.

The **cash flow statement** starts with the cash from the preceding balance sheet and updates it for all inflows and outflows of cash. The sales budget, cost of goods sold budget, selling and administrative expense budget, and special cash inflow and cash outflow items are combined to determine the ending cash balance the company can anticipate at the end of the coming budget period.

Using the net income from the budgeted income statement, managers can update the equity accounts for the **budgeted balance sheet.** Building on the balance sheet for the period just past, new inventory amounts can be computed from previous budgets, purchased or sold equipment amounts can be used to adjust the fixed asset accounts, borrowed amounts can be added and paid loans can be subtracted, new balances in accounts receivable and accounts payable can be derived from unpaid amounts on the sales budget and the purchases budget, and cash from the cash budget all combine to derive the balance sheet.

LO 6: Integrate the operating budget into the overall management process.

During the budgeting process, managers must always be conscious of **the need to align the budget with the goals and objectives of the company's strategic plan**. The strategic plan provides direction for the company and must, therefore, be constantly referenced to assure that activities are supporting that plan. The budget operationalizes the plan, and the plan provides focus for the budget. They must be taken together to assure the company of achieving its goals.

LO 7: Analyze budget variances.

Without evaluating adherence to the budget, the company cannot improve either the management of the business or the budgeting process itself. Thus, the final step in each period's budgeting process requires that a **budget performance report** be prepared and analyzed. Differences between actual results and budgeted amounts are called **budget variances.** Positive amounts indicate the actual amount exceeded budget while negative amounts indicate budgeted items were higher. Until the specific item is known, however, the desirability of positive or negative measures cannot be assessed. In general positive variances for inflows and negative variances for outflows are considered best; however, even this rule cannot be deemed universally true. Investigation into the cause of the variance must be undertaken to make a true judgment.

Appendix:

Manufacturing companies may utilize a standard cost system to provide a benchmark for quantities to be used and prices to be paid for resources. **Variance analysis** provides a methodology to isolate the variances caused by usage from the variances caused by price. Each item will have a standard amount of resource which should be used in its manufacture and a standard amount that should be paid per unit of resource. Differences from these standards are isolated and analyzed to determine the cause of the deviations. Variances should be computed at the earliest possible point in the process so that problems can be identified early and corrected.

The **direct materials price variance** examines the difference between actual price paid for a quantity of materials and the standard price expected to be paid. The **direct materials quantity variance** holds the price constant (by using the standard price) and finding the variance caused by differences in material actually used and the amount that should have been used for the actual amount of units produced (The amount that should have been used is computed as actual output of units times the standard quantity per unit.).

A similar calculation examines labor variances. The actual amount paid for labor compared with the standard amount that should have been paid for the hours worked yields the **direct labor rate variance.** As with the materials, the standard amount of labor that should have been used for the actual output compared with the amount of labor that was used yields the **direct labor efficiency variance.**

If the company management feels that incurrence of variable overhead aligns most closely with direct labor hours, then the difference between hours actually worked and the standard hours that should have been worked can be used to compute the **variable manufacturing overhead efficiency variance.** The difference in standard hours and actual hours times the standard variable overhead rate will yield this variance. A difference between actual variable overhead and the standard variable overhead for actual direct labor hours worked provides the **variable overhead spending variance.**

The **fixed manufacturing overhead volume variance** relates to utilization of the fixed-cost resource. The difference between plant capacity units and actual units produced yields over- or under-production. That over- or under-production amount times the direct labor efficiency standard yields the standard direct labor hours for over- or under-production. Those standard direct labor hours for over- or under-production times the standard fixed overhead rate gives the fixed overhead volume variance. The **fixed overhead budget variance** is simply the difference between budgeted fixed overhead and actual fixed overhead.

A **performance report** showing of all of the favorable variances and the unfavorable variances provides information to management for use in evaluating the processes. Large variances will need to be investigated and, perhaps, remedied.

CHAPTER GLOSSARY

Bill of material: a listing of the quantity and description of each direct material item used to produce one unit

Bottom-up budgeting: an approach to budgeting for which lower level managers and employees prepare the initial budget

Budget variance: the difference between the actual and budgeted amounts for a budget category

Budgeted balance sheet: a presentation of estimated assets, liabilities, and owners' equity at the end of the budget period

Internal Planning and Measurement Tools

Budgeted cash flow statement: a statement of a company's expected sources and uses of cash during the budget period

Budgeted income statement: a pro forma income statement that shows the expected net income for the budgeted period

Budgeted performance report: a report that compares the actual amounts spent against the budgeted amounts for a budget category

Cash budget: a budget that shows whether the expected amount of cash operating activities generate will be sufficient to pay anticipated expenses during the budget period

Cash payments schedule: a schedule that details the amount of cash a company expects to pay out during the budget period

Cash receipts schedule: a schedule that details the amount of cash a company expects to collect during the budget period from the sales of its product

Cost of goods sold budget: a budget that calculates the total cost of all the products a company estimates it will sell during the budget period (also called a cost of services budget for a service business)

Cost of services budget: a budget that calculates the total cost of all the products a company estimates it will sell during the budget period (also called a cost of goods sold budget for a merchandising company)

Direct labor efficiency standard: the estimated number of direct labor hours required to produce one unit

Direct labor efficiency variance: a variance that measures whether production consumed more or less than the standard direct labor hours to manufacture the actual quantity produced during the month

Direct labor rate standard: the expected hourly wage paid to production workers

Direct labor rate variance: a variance that measures the effect of unanticipated wage rate changes by calculating the difference between the actual wage rate paid to employees and the direct labor rate standard

Direct material price standard: the anticipated price to be paid for each direct material item

Direct material quantity standard: the amount of direct material required to make one unit of product

Direct material quantity variance: the difference between the standard and actual consumption of direct material for the number of units actually manufactured

Direct material price variance: the difference between the amount the company expected to pay for direct material and the amount it actually paid

Empower: to give employees the authority to make decisions concerning their job responsibilities, including decisions about items in the operating budget

Fixed manufacturing overhead budget variance: a variance that measures the difference between actual total fixed manufacturing overhead and the budgeted fixed manufacturing overhead

Fixed manufacturing overhead volume variance: a variance that measures utilization of plant capacity

Forecasted financial statements: financial statements that estimate what may happen in the future instead of what actually happened from past transactions (Also called pro forma financial statements)

Imposed budget: a budget for which upper management sets budget amounts for all operating activities with little possibility of negotiation

Incremental budgeting: the process of using the prior year's budget or the company's actual results to build the new operating budget

Master budget: the plan for a firm's operating activities for a specified period of time (also called the operating budget)

Operating budget: the plan for a firm's operating activities for a specified period of time (also called a master budget)

Participative budget: a budget approach in which managers and employees at many levels of the company are engaged in setting performance standards and preparing the budget

Perpetual budgeting: a budgeting approach management uses so that as one month ends, another month's budget is added to the end of the budget so that, at any time, the budget projects 12 months into the future (also called rolling budgeting)

Pro forma financial statements: financial statements that estimate what may happen in the future instead of what actually happened in the past (also called forecasted financial statements)

Production budget: a budget which plans for the cost and number of units that must be manufactured to meet the sales forecast and the desired quantity of ending finished goods inventory

Purchases budget: a budget which plans for the cost and number of units that must be purchased to meet the sales forecast and the desired quantity of ending finished goods inventory

Rolling budgeting: a budgeting approach management uses so that as one month ends, another month's budget is added to the end of the budget so that, at any time, the budget projects 12 months into the future (also called perpetual budgeting)

Sales budget: a budget that details the expected sales revenue from a company's primary operating activities during the budget period

Sales forecast: the prediction of sales for the budget period

Selling and administrative expense budget: a budget that calculates all costs other than the cost of products or services required to support a company's forecasted sales

Standard direct labor cost: the total expected cost of labor used to produce one unit of product, calculated by multiplying the direct labor efficiency standard by the direct labor rate standard

Standard direct material cost: the total expected cost of each material used to produce one unit, calculated by multiplying the standard quantity of direct material by the standard price

Standard fixed manufacturing overhead rate: an overhead rate calculated by dividing the budgeted fixed manufacturing overhead cost by the appropriate cost driver

Standard fixed overhead cost: the expected fixed overhead cost to produce one unit, calculated by multiplying the standard fixed manufacturing overhead rate by the direct labor efficiency standard

Standard variable manufacturing overhead rate: an overhead rate calculated by dividing the budgeted variable overhead cost to produce one unit, calculated by multiplying the standard variable manufacturing overhead rate by the direct labor efficiency standard

Standard variable overhead cost: the expected variable overhead cost to produce one unit, calculated by multiplying the standard variable manufacturing overhead rate by the direct labor efficiency standard

Top-down budgeting: an approach to budgeting in which senior executives prepare the budget, and lower level managers and employees work to meet that budget

Variable manufacturing overhead efficiency variance: a variance that measures the difference between the variable manufacturing overhead cost attributable to planned and actual direct labor hours worked

Variable manufacturing overhead spending variance: a variance that measures the difference between what was actually spent on variable manufacturing overhead and what should have been spend, based on the actual direct labor hours worked

Zero-based budgeting: an approach to budgeting where managers start from zero when preparing a new budget, and they must justify each item on the budget every year as though it were a new budget item

PROBLEM APPLICATIONS

Multiple Choice Questions:

For each of the following multiple choice questions, circle the letter of the BEST response.

1. Which of the following budgets would be prepared last?
   a. Sales budget
   b. Cash budget
   c. Purchases budget
   d. Budgeted balance sheet

2. An advantage of bottom-up budgeting is that
   a. employees must take time from their work to provide input on the budget.
   b. top management is more aware of company goals.
   c. employees may try to pad the budget.
   d. employees feel like part of the company team.

3. Incremental budgeting
   a. uses the prior year's budget to build the current year's budget.
   b. starts from zero when preparing a new budget.
   c. adds another month's budget to the end of the existing budget so that, at any given time, the budget projects twelve months into the future.
   d. reduces the budget by a specified increment each period.

4. Budgeting can help a company
   a. establish standards.
   b. meet deadlines.

      c. evaluate personnel.
      d. identify needed equipment.

5. For the month of November, McGee and Company budgeted $20,000 for payroll expenses, $16,000 for selling expenses, $8,000 for administrative expenses, $2,000 for depreciation expense, $4,000 for other expenses and $10,000 for purchases. Expenses are paid the month incurred while purchases are paid the month following the purchase. If purchases in October were $12,000, what cash payments are expected for the month of November?
      a. $60,000
      b. $62,000
      c. $70,000
      d. $72,000

6. The ending cash balance on a cash budget equals
      a. beginning balance minus cash receipts plus cash payments plus borrowing minus repayments
      b. cash receipts minus cash payments
      c. beginning balance plus cash receipts minus cash payments minus repayments
      d. beginning balance plus cash receipts minus cash payments plus borrowing minus repayments

7. The main advantage of perpetual budgeting is that
      a. the budget preparation process becomes so routine that employees do not have to spend a lot of time preparing it.
      b. it spreads the workload for a budget preparation evenly over the year allowing employees to incorporate budgeting into their normal monthly work schedule.
      c. waste in the budget will not be simply rolled over into the next month's budget.
      d. forces managers to re-examine the items included in the budget and justify their continuation.

8. Top-down budgets
      a. generally take more time to prepare than using the bottom-up approach.
      b. include the working knowledge of daily activities.
      c. are prepared with company goals in mind.
      d. encourage employee acceptance.

9. Which of the following factors can cause the sales forecast to be too high?
      a. a strong economy
      b. increase in competitor price

c. development of a substitute product

d. bankruptcy of a major competitor

10. A cash budget will

    a. show the total expenses the company will take in the coming accounting period.

    b. reveal whether a company should expect a need for short-term external financing during the budget period.

    c. show the exact amount of cash the company will have at the end of the period.

    d. help with determining whether additional personnel need to be hired.

11. A budgeted balance sheet

    a. shows expected cash inflows.

    b. yields expected net income.

    c. has assets equal to liabilities plus equity

    d. brings forward the fixed asset amounts from the preceding period.

12. What type of business would have neither a production or purchases budget?

    a. Merchandising.

    b. Service.

    c. Hybrid.

    d. Manufacturing

13. A change in the sales budget would always

    a. cause changes in all of the other budgets.

    b. mean less money coming into the company.

    c. require the hiring of more sales people.

    d. lead to increased commissions for sales people.

14. The calculation of expected purchases is similar to the

    a. determination of personnel to hire.

    b. computation of cost of goods sold.

    c. calculation of expected cash receipts.

    d. determination of expected sales dollars.

15. Variances measure differences between

    a. real and budgeted amounts.

    b. actual and standard amounts.

    c. true and estimated amounts.

    d. budgeted and estimated amounts.

True / False Questions:

1. A benefit of budgeting is that it assists the organization in resource allocation.

2. The cash receipts schedule details the amount of cash a company expects to pay out during the budget period.
3. Budget variances are differences between different budgeted amounts.
4. Incremental budgeting may lead to a "use it or lose it" philosophy among managers.
5. The sales forecast is the basis for all other budgeted amounts.
6. A purchases budget is generally used by a manufacturer while a production budget is generally used by a merchandiser.
7. A selling and administrative expense budget calculates all costs, other than the cost of products or services, required to support a company's forecasted sales.
8. One of the most important budgeting functions is for top management to ensure that each budget aligns with the goals and objectives of the strategic plan.
9. Most firms require managers to prepare or review a budget performance report that compares the actual amounts against the budgeted amounts for a budget category.
10. Budget variances are the results of a flaw in the budgeting process.
11. The goal of using standard costing is to generate positive variances.
12. Zero-based budgeting saves time because the old budget does not need to be reviewed
13. Top-down budgeting allows managers to provide employees with budgeting experience.
14. The master budget is a series of multiple budgets that work together.
15. Depreciation expense must be excluded from the cash budget because it is not a cash item.

Matching: Match each numbered item with the appropriate letter.

_____	1	Perpetual budgeting
_____	2	Imposed budget
_____	3	Operating budget
_____	4	Top-down budgeting
_____	5	Incremental budgeting

_____	6	Zero-based budgeting
_____	7	Forecasted financial statements
_____	8	Budgeted income statement
_____	9	Bottom-up budgeting
_____	10	Budgeted cash flow statement

A   estimates what may happen in the future instead of what actually happened from past transactions.

B   top executive prepare the budget, and lower-level managers and employees work to meet that budget.

C   upper management sets amounts for all operating activities with little responsibility of negotiation.

D   the plan for a firm's operating activities for a specified period of time.

E   starts from scratch, or zero, when preparing a new budget and managers must justify each item on the budget every year as though it were a brand new item.

F   shows the expected net income for the period.

G   statement of a company's expected sources and uses of cash during the budget period.

H   as one month ends, another month's budget is added to the end of the budget so that, at any given time, the budget projects twelve months into the future.

I   lower level managers and employees prepare the initial budget.

J   the process of using the prior year's budget or the company's actual results to build the new operating budget.

Exercises:

1. Castle, Inc. produces guitars. In the last quarter of 2003, the company expects to sell 200 units in October, 185 units in November and 275 units in December at $350 each. Prepare a sales budget for the company.

2. The Westmoreland Company has budgeted sales of $93,000 for 2003 and budgeted cost of goods sold of $74,000. In addition, the company anticipates 2003 operating expenses to be $13,000, interest expense to be $800 and taxes to be $1,000. Prepare a budgeted income statement for the company.

3. Home Industries expects 2004 sales for January, February, and March to be $200,000, $275,000, and $310,000 respectively. The company expects that 70% of the sales will be in cash while the remaining 30% will be on account and collected in the month following the sale.
   a.   Assuming the company's sales from the previous December were $175,000, prepare a cash receipts schedule for the first quarter of 2004.
   b.   What would be the balance in Accounts Receivable at the end of the quarter?

4. Patty's Pies makes double-deep fried fruit pies; standards pertaining to the production of one case of pies specify that a case of pies will require 4 hours at $13 per hour.. The company incurred direct labor costs of $46,460 based on 4,250 hours worked.
   a.   What is the direct labor rate variance?
   b.   If production indicated that 4,200 hours should have been worked, what is the direct labor efficiency variance?

5. Leonard, Inc. manufactures home collectibles. The standards pertaining to the production of one of the company's products indicate that 7 pounds of raw materials should be used at $5.90 per pound for each unit of product. The company actually produced 1,200 units of product and used 7,800 pounds of raw materials at a total cost of $54,600.
   a.   What is the raw materials quantity variance?
   b.   The company had purchased all of the material used this period. What is the price variance?

6. Joe's Joint has the following information:
   Actual fixed overhead cost $240,620
   Budgeted fixed overhead $230,000
   Actual number of direct labor hours   22,000
   Fixed overhead rate $11.50 per direct labor hour
   Fixed overhead for actual production $241, 500
   a.   Determine the fixed overhead budget variance.
   b.   Determine the fixed overhead volume variance.

Problems:

The Beverly Company plans to sell the following quantities of wagons:

September 400
October 500
November 650
December 850
January 300

The company buys each unit for $30 and sells each unit for $45. The company had 30 units on hand at the beginning of October and plans to have ending inventory each month equal to 30% of the next month's sales. Seventy percent of the company's sales are on a cash basis while the remainder is made on account with collection made in the month following the sale. The company expects operating expenses to be 20% of sales.

Prepare a purchases budget, budgeted income statement and a cash receipts budget for October through December.

SOLUTIONS

Multiple Choice:

1. D
2. D
3. A
4. A
5. A
6. D
7. B
8. C
9. C
10. B
11. C
12. B
13. A
14. B
15. B

True / False:

1. True
2. False; the cash receipts schedule details the amount of cash a company expects to collect during the budget period.
3. False; budget variances are difference between actual results and the budget.
4. True
5. True
6. False; a purchases budget is generally used by a merchandiser while a production budget is generally used by a manufacturer.
7. True
8. True
9. True
10. False; regardless of the care taken with the budget process, variance will likely occur
11. False; the goal of standard costing is to provide a benchmark
12. False; zero-based budget increases time because each item starts at zero.
13. False; top-down budgeting leaves the employees out of the budgeting process.
14. True
15. True

Matching:

1.	H
2.	C
3.	D
4.	B
5.	J
6.	E
7.	A
8.	F
9.	I
10.	G

Exercises:

1.

Castle, Inc.
Sales Budget
for the year ended 2003

	October	November	December	Total
Sales in Units	200	185	275	660
Unit Sales Price	$350	$350	$350	$350
Sales in Dollars	$70,000	$64,750	$96,250	$231,000

2.

Westmoreland Company
Budgeted Income Statement
For the year ended 2003

Sales	$93,000
Cost of Goods Sold	74,000
Gross Profit	$19,000
Operating Expenses	13,000
Interest Expense	800
Tax Expense	1,000
Net Income	$4,200

3a.

Home Industries
Cash Receipts Schedule
For the Quarter Ended March, 2004

	January	February	March
Cash Sales	$140,000	$192,500	$217,000
Collections from previous month	52,500	60,000	82,500
Total Budgeted Receipts	$192,500	$252,500	$299,500

b. Accounts Receivable balance $310,000 x 30% = $93,000

4a.	Actual hours x actual price	$46,460
	Actual hours x standard price	55,250
	Rate variance	$ 8,790 Favorable
b.	Actual hours x standard price	$55,250
	Standard hours x standard price	54,600
	Efficiency variance	$ 650 Unfavorable
5a.	Actual qty. x standard price	$46,020
	Standard qty x standard price	49,560 (8,400 pounds @ $5.90)
	Quantity variance	$ 3,540 Favorable
b.	Actual qty. x actual price	$54,600
	Actual qty. x standard price	46,020
	Price variance	$ 8,580 Unfavorable
6a.	Actual	$240,620
	Budgeted	230,000
	Budget variance	$ 10,620 Unfavorable
b.	Budgeted	$230,000
	Standard qty. x standard price	241,500
	Volume variance	$ 11,.500 Favorable

Problems:

Purchases Budget

	October	November	December
Unit sales	500	650	850
+ Desired ending inventory	195	255	90
- Beginning inventory	30	195	255
= Purchases in units	665	710	685

Budgeted Income Statement

	October	November	December
Sales	$22,500	$29,250	$38,250
Cost of Goods Sold	15,000	19,500	25,500
Gross Profit	$7,500	$9,750	$12,750
Operating Expenses	4,500	5,850	7,650
Net Income	$3,000	$3,900	$5,100

Cash Receipts Budget

	October	November	December
Cash sales	$15,750	$20,475	$26,775
Collections from previous month	5,400	6,750	8,775
Total cash receipts	$21,150	$27,225	$35,550

Chapter 11
Internal Allocation
of Scarce Resources

CHAPTER SUMMARY

The expenditure of large amounts for long-lived, high-dollar items in a company must be undertaken with more caution than the decision to purchase an everyday item like inventory. Because the amounts are so large and the company becomes tied to the decision for and extended period of time, the process by which managers enter such acquisitions is more complex and cautious than with smaller items. This process, called the capital budgeting process, leads to decisions about acquiring, replacing, or eliminating these large, expensive items.

LO 1: Explain the process of capital budgeting.

The capital budget takes a relatively long-range perspective. **Looking forward five or ten years, or perhaps even longer, managers project plans for acquisition of buildings, machinery, land, and other capital assets. Not only must the promise of future benefit be present in these expenditures, but they must further the company's strategic goals.**

These expensive assets must exceed **a threshold set by management and must extend for a relatively long period of time.** When the price threshold and time period tests are met, however, the assets, when purchased, appear on the company's financial statements as a long-term asset. This asset, then, will be used up over the time period it is expected to last.

LO 2: Delineate the four shared characteristics of all capital

Four characteristics distinguish capital projects. They have **long lives**, generally five to ten years or longer. They also carry a **high cost** for the company. In general, once the acquisition is made, the company becomes "locked in" to the decision because recovery of the investment is difficult if not impossible. These **sunk costs** become investments that the company must simply accept. Last, capital projects carry **a high degree of risk**, primarily due to the high cost that is a sunk cost for the company. An error in the evaluation of such a project becomes extremely costly to the company. The high risk of the projects leads managers to exercise a great deal of caution in making these decisions.

LO 3: Describe the cost of capital and the concept of scarce

Money that is not working is really of little use to the holder. Although that statement sounds REALLY wrong, the idea is sound. Imagine having money on a desert island. Paper money is simply paper. This basic idea ties to the idea of the cost of capital. Unless investors earn something on their money, they are probably unwilling to let someone have that money. The idea that money can earn more money means that investments have a cost. They should return something to the investor in excess of the amount paid for them. That extra amount that should be returned is the **cost of capital**, also called the **required rate of return.**

The return required on capital projects must be adequate to satisfy both debt holders and stockholders of companies since both contribute to the financing used to acquire long-term assets in a company. The combined cost of debt and equity financing is a weighted average called the **blended cost of capital.** Each financing method's required return is weighted by the proportion of the total financing each provides to the company. Interest provides the return to debt holders while the combination of dividends and stock appreciation provides the return to equity holders.

Unfortunately, few people in the world and few companies have the luxury of having all of the money each could possibly need or want. Thus, the investment funds are restricted to the best uses possible. These limited funds, known generally as **scarce resources,** restrict the projects in which companies can invest and require that they search for the projects that promise the best return.

LO 4: Determine the information relevant to a capital budgeting decision.

The capital budgeting process involves four steps. These steps are designed to gather and evaluate the relevant information in order that that project(s) selected will be good for the company. As a first step, the company members **(1) identify capital projects**. More projects exist than can be accepted so the vital part of the process lies in the second step. Company personnel **(2) determine relevant cash flows**. As with the decisions in Chapter 9, including all estimated inflows and outflows over the life of the project must be accomplished to evaluate accurately. Only those **future** cash flows which **differ among choices** are relevant to the decision. Once all relevant cash flows are gathered, company personnel must **(3) select a method of evaluation.** These methods provide the primary information in this chapter. Lastly, the company management must **(4) evaluate the alternatives** and, hopefully, select the best one(s).

LO 5: Evaluate potential capital investments using three capital budgeting decision models: payback method, net present value, and the internal rate of return.

Several evaluation methods are available for use in capital budgeting decisions. The **payback period method** provides an easy and straight-forward method of doing a simple check on a project. The initial investment divided by annual net cash inflow provides the time required for the project to "pay back" the initial investment. A project with uneven cash flows requires that each year's cash inflow be subtracted from the initial investment until the investment amount is "returned" through cash flows. Payback focuses on liquidity of an investment and often serves as an initial screen. It does not, however, incorporate the idea of the time value of money.

The second and third methods discussed do incorporate the time value of money. These discounted cash flow methods utilize the idea that money held today provides more value than money to be received later since today's money can be invested to give us a return and, therefore, provide us with more money. These methods reduce the value of future money by the amount of return we expect on our investments.

A second budgeting decision model is called the **net present value (NPV)** method of evaluation. Managers discount (reduce by the amount of interest earned or paid between the current point and the future point at which the cash flow will occur) all cash inflows and cash outflows and then net the inflows with outflows. Discounting brings all cash flow amounts from their future value to their value today (future value less the interest amount that would be earned or paid on the cash). Since the required return on investment is being "built in" by the discounting, an NPV of zero or above indicates the project is acceptable to the company. This model's weakness lies in the fact that it does not discriminate among acceptable projects; it only lets us know if the project meets or exceeds the required return we have set.

The **profitability index** yields the actual rate of return of the project and thereby lets the company managers determine which project is "better" in the return it provides. The profitability index divides the present value of cash inflows by the present value of the outflows. The resulting index can be used to rank projects in terms of preference. A higher index indicates a more preferred project. The profitability index can be used in conjunction with the net present value calculations.

The third method of evaluating lies in finding the **internal rate of return (IRR)** of a project. This method provides the evaluator with an estimate of the actual percentage return expected from the project. The calculations yield a percentage return. A simple project with no residual value and even cash flows can be computed by dividing the initial outlay by the expected annual inflow (return). The calculation provides a factor which can then be looked up on a present value of an annuity table. More complex projects require the use of a financial calculator to find the return.

Regardless of evaluation method, however, all projects must meet four criteria. First, the projects must align with the strategic goals of the company. Second, employees involved with a project must accept it. Otherwise, employees, either deliberately or inadvertently, can sabotage the project. A third requirement lies in the need for realistic estimates of cost, inflows, and savings. Bad data during the estimation period can cost companies extremely high amounts of money. Fourth, companies should avoid projects which provide rewards to selected personnel, especially advocates of the project. They are apt to be biased and may generate inaccurate information.

Appendix:

LO 6: Explain the concept of simple interest and compound interest and describe the concept of an annuity.

Almost everyone remembers the calculation of interest from grade school where everyone learned that interest equals principal times rate times time. This calculation assumes that only the initial amount invested can earn interest. When no money is earned on the interest itself, only on the initial investment, this is known as **simple interest.**

A more common situation in business today occurs when interest is earned (or incurred) on previous interest amounts. When the interest is earned on interest, this is called **compound interest**—the interest keeps compounding by being added onto other interest. If interest is left in a savings account, for example, the bank will compute the total amount in the account (including interest paid previously) to determine current period interest.

Future values are the amounts that include interest either already earned or which will be earned on an investment for a specific period of time at a specific interest rate which is compounded at specific intervals. Present value indicates the amount before any interest is added.

Many cash flows in business occur on a regular basis—payments on equipment, cars, buildings, and so forth. When a regular cash flow occurs, whether the cash is received or paid, the cash flow is called an **annuity**, and the regular cash flow is called a rent.

> **LO 7: Determine present and future values using present and future value tables.**

Rather than compute interest each period, constantly adding in the preceding interest, we have available a wonderful aid called present and future value tables. These tables provide "factors" which can be applied to amounts to determine the information you are trying to compute. When a person is using the table, some important formulas to remember for single amounts are the following:

Present value = Future value x Present value factor   AND
Future value = Present value x Future value factor.

The factor is always from the table of the variable you are trying to find (present value or future value), and it is found at the intersection of the interest rate and the compounding periods. Investors may provide money (or receive money—the direction of the cash flow will not affect our computations.) at one point in time. A single cash flow's present or future value can be computed by using the tables labeled as "…value of $1 table."

Alternatively, when a cash flow occurs once every compounding period, the cash flow is known as an **annuity.** Annuities are common in business because many payments occur regularly—payments such as payments on vehicles, payments on leased equipment, and so forth. Annuities must be for the same amount each period and must occur at the same points at which compounding occurs. Annuities, in present value terminology, are called "rents." Again, the direction of the cash flow does not matter for purposes of calculation. The important formulas to remember in applying annuity table factors are the following:

Present value of an annuity = Rent x Present value of an annuity factor   AND
Future value of an annuity = Rent x Future value of an annuity factor.

Again, the factor is always from the table of the variable you are trying to find.

Since interest rates are stated on an annual basis, some adjustment may be required when more than one compounding period occurs per year. In such a case, the annual interest rate is divided by the number of compounding periods while the number of years is multiplied by the number of compounding periods.

CHAPTER GLOSSARY

Annuity: a stream of cash flows where the dollar amount of each payment and the time interval between each payment are uniform

Blended cost of capital: the combined cost of debt and equity financing

Capital budget: the budget that outlines how a firm intends to allocate its scarce resources over a 5-year, 10-year, or even longer period

Capital budgeting: the planning and decision process for making investments in capital projects

Capital assets: long-lived assets such as land, buildings, machinery, and equipment

Capital investments: business expenditures made to acquire expensive assets that will be used for more than one year (also called capital projects)

Capital projects: business expenditures made to acquire expensive assets that will be used for more than one year (also called capital investments)

Compound interest: interest calculated on the investment principal plus all previously earned interest at the end of each compounding period

Compounding: determining the future value of an amount invested today

Compounding period: the frequency that interest is calculated and added to the principal, such as annually, semiannually, quarterly, monthly, or daily

Cost of capital: the cost of obtaining financing from all available financing sources (also called the required rate of return or the hurdle rate)

Cost of debt capital: the interest a company pays to its creditors

Cost of equity capital: the return equity investors expect to earn, combining dividends received and the appreciation in the market value of the stock

Discounting: determining the present value of an amount of cash to be received in the future

Discounting cash flows: determining the present value of cash to be received in future periods

Future value: the value of a payment, or series of payments, at a future point in time, calculated with an interest rate

Hurdle rate: the cost of obtaining financing from all available financing sources (also called the cost of capital or the required rate of return)

Internal rate of return (IRR): the calculated expected percentage return promised by the project

Net cash flow: the project's expected cash inflows minus its cash outflows for a specific period

Net present value (NPV): the present value of cash inflows minus the present value of cash outflows associated with a capital budgeting project

Payback period method: a capital budgeting technique that measures the length of time a capital project must generate positive net cash flows that equal, or "pay back," the original investment in the project

Present value (PV) of a project: the amount the future cash inflows is worth today when discounted at the appropriate discount rate

Present value (PV) of an investment: the amount an investment is worth today evaluated at the appropriate interest rate

Profitability index: an index of the values of alternative but acceptable capital budgeting projects, whose index values we calculate by dividing the present value of the project's cash inflows by the present value of its cash outflows

Relevant net cash flows: future cash flows that differ among decision alternatives

Required rate of return: the cost of obtaining financing from all available financing sources (also called the cost of capital or the hurdle rate)

Scarce resources: the limited amount of funding available to spend on capital projects

Simple interest: interest calculated only on the original principal

Sunk costs: costs that cannot be recovered

Time value of money: the increase in the value of cash over time due to the accumulation of investment income

PROBLEM APPLICATIONS

Multiple Choice Questions:

For each of the following multiple choice questions, circle the letter of the BEST response.

1. Capital projects are generally
   a. short-lived.
   b. low cost.
   c. certain in terms of return.
   d. tied to the strategic plan.

2. A company's blended cost of capital
   a. includes the cost of debt capital adjusted for risk
   b. includes the cost of equity capital adjusted for risk
   c. includes a combined cost of debt and equity.
   d. includes a combined cost of debt and equity adjusted for risk.

3. Below are the steps in a typical capital project evaluation:
   1. Select a method of evaluating the alternatives
   2. Determine the relevant cash flows for alternative projects
   3. Identify possible projects
   4. Evaluate the alternatives and select the capital project to be funded

   Which of the following list the steps in the proper order?
   a. 1, 2, 3, 4
   b. 3, 2, 1, 4
   c. 3, 1, 2, 4
   d. 2, 3, 1, 4

4. If a capital project is expected to generate additional cash inflows of $50,000, but will require additional cash outflows of $20,000, what is the net cash flow for the project?
   a. $20,000.
   b. $30,000.
   c. $50,000.
   d. $70,000.

5. The payback period method of evaluating capital projects ignores
    a. the time value of money.
    b. cash inflows.
    c. the liquidity of the project.
    d. uneven cash flows.

6. The management of Murphy Enterprises is considering a capital project that will require an initial investment of $25,000 and is expected to generate annual net cash inflows of $4,500. The payback period in years for this project is
    a. 0.2
    b. 1.0
    c. 5.1
    d. 5.6

7. Kennedy and Company is considering expanding the company's operations by purchasing an additional distribution center for its operations. The purchase price of the distribution center is $350,000 and the company expects it to generate annual cash inflows of $40,000 for 20 years. If the project has a zero salvage value and the company's cost of capital is 8%, the net present value of the project is
    a. (178,400)
    b. 42,724
    c. 392,724
    d. 1,480,480

8. Johnson, Inc. has decided to purchase a new machine for its processing plant which cost $80,000. The company estimated that the machine will generate net cash flows of $22,039 over its useful life of 4 years after which time it will be worthless. The internal rate of return on the vehicle?
    a. 2%
    b. 3%
    c. 4%
    d. 5%

9. Melvin, Inc. is considering a capital investment that costs $18,000, has a useful life of 5 years and would generate annual cash inflows of $4,000. If the company has a cost of capital of 8 percent, the project's profitability index is
    a. 1.10
    b. 1.07
    c. 0.90
    d. 0.89

10. Below is information for four projects being reviewed by the Encore Company:

	Payback Period	Net Present Value	Profitability Index
Project A	2.4	500	1.05
Project B	2.4	300	1.08
Project C	2.1	200	1.04
Project D	3.5	0	1.02

If Encore can invest in any of the projects, which one(s) should the company select?
a. Project A.
b. Project B.
c. All of them.
d. All but D.

11. Susan's Shoppe has $100,000 in debt which has a cost of 15%. The cost of equity is 18%, and equity totals $400,000. Susan's blended cost of capital is
a. 14%.
b. 14.7%.
c. 17.4%.
d. 17.8%.

12. Susan's Shoppe has $100,000 in debt which has a cost of 15%. The cost of equity is 18%, and equity totals $400,000. Susan needs another $100,000 to finance expansion of her Shoppe, and the banker tells her that the interest rate on the new debt will be 12%, what will the new blended cost of capital?
a. 13%.
b. 14.7%.
c. 16%.
d. 16.5%.

13. George's Garage owner wants to buy a new computer to test motors. George estimates that his required rate of return is 10%, and that the machine will last 5 years. The net present value of the project is zero. This outcome tells George
a. the project's outcome is not clear.
b. the project actual return cannot be computed.
c. the project's return is exactly 10%.
d. the project will cause him to lose money.

14. An annuity of $1,000 per year received for 5 years at an interest rate of 8% will provide
    a. a total of $5,000.00.
    b. a total of $5,400.00.
    c. a total of $8,052.50.
    d. a total of $5,866.60.

15. If a company's management decides to accept a capital project, it should be
    a. championed by people who will benefit the most.
    b. compatible with the company's strategic goals.
    c. the lowest risk project available.
    d. a project that won the monetary reward offered for the best idea.

True / False Questions:

1. All long-lived assets should be capitalized and depreciated over their useful lives.
2. Capital assets usually include items such as land, buildings and equipment.
3. Cost of capital is also referred to as the required rate of return or the hurdle rate.
4. The cost of equity capital is simply the return equity investors expect to earn from the appreciation in the market value of the stock.
5. When using the payback period method of evaluating capital projects, the project with the highest resulting calculation should be selected.
6. Most managers use the payback method as a screening device after establishing a maximum payback period for potential projects.
7. The net present value method of evaluating capital projects is the only method that includes time value of money.
8. If a lower discount rate is used, the net present value of a project will be larger than if a higher discount rate is used.
9. If a project has a higher profitability index than another project, it must have higher expected cash flows as well.
10. If a capital project has an IRR below the company's cost of capital it will have a negative net present value.
11. A good way to encourage employees to look for good projects is to offer an incentive for the best projects found.
12. Interest expense can be deducted on a company's income statement, but dividends on equity cannot.
13. If a project has a high degree of risk, it should be avoided.
14. Most companies have more capital project opportunities than they can accept.
15. The idea of the time value of money relates to the ability of money to accumulate investment income over time.

Matching:

Match each numbered term with its lettered definition.

_____ 1 Internal rate of return (IRR)	_____ 6 Payback period method
_____ 2 Capital budget	_____ 7 Compound interest
_____ 3 Profitability index	_____ 8 Capital investments
_____ 4 Net present value (NPV)	_____ 9 Compounding period
_____ 5 Cost of capital	_____ 10 annuity

A   business expenditures made to acquire expensive assets that will be used for more than one year

B   A stream of cash flows where the dollar amount of each payment and the time interval between each payment are uniform.

C   the budget that outlines how a firm intends to allocate its scare resources over a five-year, ten-year, or even longer time period.

D   is the present value of cash inflows minus the present value of cash outflows associated with a capital budgeting project.

E   the cost of obtaining financing from all available financing sources.

F   is the frequency that interest is calculated and added to the principal

G   a capital budgeting technique that measures the length of time a capital project must generate positive net cash flows that equal the original investment

H   is interest calculated on the investment principal plus all previously earned interest at the end of each compounding period.

I   is an index of the values of alternate capital budgeting projects calculated by dividing the present value of each project's cash inflows by the present value of its cash outflows.

J   is the calculated expected percentage return promised by the project.

Internal Allocation of Scarce Resources

Exercises:

1. The Ranger Company has $340,000 in total assets, $119,000 in total liabilities and $221,000 in total equity. The cost of financing is 8% for the debt and 12% for the equity. Calculate the company's blended cost of capital.

2. Masser, Inc. is considering purchasing a vending machine for the lobby of its office building. The machine will cost $5,000; in addition, products for the machine will cost $0.75 each and will be sold for $1.00 each. If the company expects to sell 300 items per month, what is the payback period in years for this investment?

3. The management of the Atlantis Company is interested in purchasing a new developing machine for its photo-processing lab. The machine costs $30,000 and is expected to generate annual cash inflows of $8,000 over its estimated 5 year useful life at which time it can be sold for $1,500. The company's cost of capital is 10%. Calculate the net present value of the machine.

4. Tip Top Taxi, Inc. has decided to invest in a new vehicle for its fleet. The company has estimated that the vehicle will generate cash flows of $4,108 during its useful life of 7 years after which time it will be worthless. If the vehicle cost $20,000, what is the internal rate of return on the vehicle?

5. Price Company is considering two different projects. Project A costs $15,000, has a useful life of 5 years, and would generate annual cash inflows of $4,000. Project B costs $12,000, has a useful life of 5 years, and would generate annual cash inflows of $3,500. Based on each project's profitability index, which project should be selected assuming the company has a cost of capital of 6 percent?

6. Poor Boys, Inc. borrowed $100,000 at 7% to buy a building. The loan will be paid in full in 30 years. Interest is paid annually and, therefore, not compounded. At the end of the 30 years, after Poor Boys pays off the loan, how much will the company have paid?

Now assume that Poor Boys had $100,000 and invested it at 7% return, compounded annually. At the end of 30 years, how much will the company have?

Problems:

1. Iced, Inc. sells snowboards and related equipment. Currently, the company purchases its products from suppliers and resells those products to its customers; however, management is considering building a new manufacturing plant so that the company can manufacture its own products. The company is considering two locations for the plant and estimated the following figures for each site:

	Site A	Site B
Cost of plant	450,000	400,000
Annual cash inflows	56,000	52,000
Estimated useful life	20	20
Salvage value	35,000	30,000
Interest rate	10%	10%

Calculate the payback period, net present value and profitability index of each project site. Which location would you recommend?

2. Managers at the local copy company are considering replacing one of its old copiers with a new one. The following information is available:

Cost of new copier	$5,200
Salvage value in 5 years	200
Salvage value of old computer now	500
Annual maintenance on new computer	600
Annual maintenance on old computer	800
Cash flows from old computer	2,500 per year
Cash flows from new computer	4,000 per year
Cost of capital	10%

Evaluate the project through a net present value calculation. Should the project be accepted?

SOLUTIONS

Multiple Choice:

1.	D	9.	D
2.	C	10.	C
3.	B	11.	C
4.	B	12.	C
5.	A	13.	C
6.	D	14.	D
7.	B	15.	B
8.	C		

True / False:

1. False; the cost/benefit and materiality constraints allow practical considerations to be taken into account for long-lived but low-cost assets. such as staplers and filing cabinets.
2. True
3. True
4. False; the cost of equity capital is the return equity investors expect to earn, combining dividends received and the appreciation in the market value of the stock.
5. False; when using the payback period method of evaluating capital projects, the project with the lowest resulting calculation should be selected.
6. True
7. False; both the net present value method and internal rate of return method for evaluating capital projects include time value of money.
8. True
9. False; if a project has a higher profitability index than another project, it must have higher present value of cash flows inflows relative to its present value of cash outflows.
10. True
11. False; incentives often encourage employees to provide exaggerated information on the project.
12. True
13. False; high risk requires a high rate of return, but the project can be undertaken if a company's management believes it is worthwhile.
14. True
15. True

Matching

1. J
2. C
3. I
4. D
5. E
6. G
7. H
8. A
9. F
10. B

Exercises

1.

Method of Financing		Proportion of Financing Provided		Cost of Financing		Weighted Cost of Financing
Debt	35%	(119,000 / 340,000)	x	8%	=	3%
Equity	65%	(221,000 / 340,000)	x	12%	=	8%
						11%

2.

Initial Investment		Annual Cash Inflow		Payback Period
5,000	/	900*	=	5.6

* (1-0.75)*(300*12)

3.

	Amount	Factor	PV
Initial investment	(30,000)	1.0000	(30,000)
Annual cash inflows	8,000	3.7908	30,326
Residual value of machine	1,500	0.6209	931
Net present value			1,257

Internal Allocation of Scarce Resources

4.

Initial Investment	=	Annual Payments	x	PVIFA
20,000	=	4,108	x	PVIFA
4.8685	=			PVIFA

IRR	=	10%

5.

	PV of inflows	/	PV of outflows	=	PI Index
Project					
A	16,850		15,000		1.12
Project B	14,743		12,000		1.23

Although Project B generates a lower annual cash inflow it requires a lower relative investment. Since Project B has a higher profitability index, it should be selected.

6. a.

$7,000 interest per year times 30 years	$210,000
Principal repayment	100,000
Total	$310,000

b.

$100,000	Principal amount
7.6123	FV factor of a single sum at 7% for 30 years
$761,230	Total

Problems

1.

	Site A	Site B
Payback period	8.04	7.69
PV of plant purchase	(450,000)	(400,000)
PV of cash inflows	476,762	442,707
PV of salvage value	5,201	4,458
Net PV	31,963	47,165
Profitability index	1.07	1.12

Although, qualitative factors should also be considered, based on the quantitative information available, Site B is a more suitable location.

2.

Cash flow	Amount	When	PV factor	PV
Purchase	($5,200)	Now	1.000	($5,200)
Salvage (new)	200	5	.6209	124
Salvage (old)	500	Now	1.000	500
Maint. savings	200	1-5	3.7908	758
Increased cash				
Flow	1,200	1-5	3.7908	5,697
		Net present value		$1,897

The project should be taken.

Chapter 12
External Financial Reporting

CHAPTER SUMMARY

The introduction you've had to financial statements has not included all of the information needed to benefit as much as possible from the information in those statements. Some additional topics in this chapter greatly increase your store of financial statement information.

> **LO 1: Characterize the importance of external financial information to financial statement users.**

Numerous types of financial statement users need the information in the financial statements of publicly traded companies. Potential investors and current shareholders examine the financial statements of companies to assess the **financial health** of the company and to try to predict the **potential for stock appreciation and dividends**. Additionally, stockholders in troubled companies want to maintain watch over their investments to **predict further problems or recovery from past problems**. A healthy company will have good cash flow, but problems with cash flow do not mean the company is doomed. While no one measure can provide a perfect (or even near perfect) method to predict the future health of a company, examination of many measures will provide a great deal of input to the data of a careful analyst. The analyst needs to consider measures of profitability, liquidity, and solvency, and examine cash flows and other special items as they arise. The stockholder who monitors these aspects of the company in which he/she is invested will stand a better chance of predicting the extent to which the company's goals align with the shareholder's goals.

Other classes of users of financial statements are the creditors who have lent money to the company, either short-term or long-term. Since short-term creditors and long-term creditors have different objectives, different parts of the financial statements are useful to them. **Short-term creditors** include trade creditors and lending institutions. These creditors **need to be assured of the profitability and liquidity** of a company to judge the company capability of paying short-term debt. **Long-term creditors also need assurance of debt-paying ability**. The difference lies in the source of the ability. Long-term creditors look for **current interest-paying ability** as well as to indicators of long-term health, such as **profitability and solvency measures**.

Regulators, though not invested in the company, serve as the **watchdogs for investors who need protection and for the general public**. Public companies must comply with specific rules and regulations in the way they do business and report. They verify that corporations and individuals pay accurate amounts of taxes on income. The **Securities and Exchange Commission (SEC)** examines reports of public companies. Its job, of course, is to monitor all public companies to check their reporting for accuracy. **Internal Revenue Service (IRS)** also monitors financial reports. Its job, of course, is to verify that corporations and individuals pay accurate amounts of taxes on income. Other, less well-known agencies also check financial information.

Ethics should, of course, be an integral part of financial reporting. Unfortunately, such is not the case. Ethics has been important in business in the past; today, too many members of management think the game is to get away with as much as possible. Once a company's reputation has been damaged by unethical behavior, however, that stigma lasts an extended time.

> **LO 2: Differentiate the valuations used for external financial reporting.**

The fact that all amounts on the financial statements are expressed in dollars (or other currencies in other countries) may hide the fact that many different types of measures are present in the statements. The basic measure is the value for which items were initially acquired. Known as **historical cost**, many items remain at this value for the time period a company holds them. However, if the value of an asset permanently declines below historical cost, the asset value must be written down through the use of an **impairment** measure. Another measure is the **net realizable value**, an amount which has been reduced to avoid overstatement of an asset such as accounts receivable. **Lower of cost or market** reduces inventory if the value of items is less than original cost. A new valuation amount for accounting is the **current market value or fair value** which is now applied to investments. This measure works for investments because market value is always available and easily verified in the business press.

An additional problem with lack of comparability of financial statements occurs because the accounting profession allows alternative methods in some of the calculations which go on the financial statements. The effects are mitigated somewhat by requirements that companies adhere to **consistency** (staying with one principle instead switching arbitrarily), **full disclosure** (providing any information relevant to decision-making), and **representational faithfulness** (avoidance of misleading the financial statement reader).

> **LO 3: Compare and contrast the straight-line and double-declining-balance methods of depreciation and the effects of each on the balance sheet and income statement.**

Among the choices allowed for companies is the choice of depreciation methods. **Depreciation measures the "using up" of long-lived assets.** Over time, the asset value is used up and becomes an expense. A significant problem occurs because the managers of a company must **estimate the expected life of the asset and the amount it will be worth when the company has used it to the extent desired**. To console those who worry excessively about these problems, the problem self-corrects at the time of disposal of the asset since the **gain or loss recognized on disposal either reduces the amount of use recognized (gain) or adds to the amount of use recognized (loss).** Gains and losses are the difference between the amount received for the asset at the time of disposal and the book value.

The most popular depreciation methods are the **straight-line** and the **double-declining-balance** methods. Straight-line takes an equal amount of use to the expense account each year. Double-declining-balance, on the other hand, applies a percentage that is double the straight-line rate to the book value of the asset each year. The Internal Revenue Service (IRS) requires a depreciation method called the **Modified Accelerated Cost Recovery System (MACRS)** for tax purposes. Since MACRS is not a generally accepted accounting principle, companies must use two different depreciation methods.

LO 4: Calculate depreciation using the straight-line and double-declining-balance methods.

The calculation of the **straight-line method** is very straight-forward. Cost of the asset less salvage value is divided by years of life to determine depreciation expense per year of the asset's life. Of course, for partial periods, the annual amount is divided to allocate to the appropriate time period.

Calculation of the double-declining-balance method is a bit more complex. The book value of the asset (cost less accumulated depreciation) always provides the declining balance since accumulated depreciation increases each year while cost remains constant. The "double" part requires that a straight-line percentage be computed then doubled. For instance, a five-year asset would be depreciated 20% per year under the straight-line method; the doubled amount would be 40%. Each year, then, the book value is multiplied times the doubled amount. However, the asset's book value can never fall below salvage. Regardless of depreciation method, though, some indication of the age of the company's assets may be determined through examination of depreciation method, depreciation expense taken on the income statement, and the information provided by the company in the footnotes to the statements.

Because most goods manufactured today are identical, application of costs to the items companies hold in inventory may prove a bit challenging. The problem is solved in accounting by making assumptions about how costs should be applied to the inventory left and to the goods that have been sold. An important aspect of this cost application issue is that the assumptions we make about cost flows have absolutely no relationship to the actual physical flow of goods.

LO 5: Compare and contrast methods of accounting for inventories and the effects of using each on the balance sheet and income statement.

The **first-in, first-out (FIFO) method** releases the first costs into the system as the cost of goods sold. The last costs in are the ones that are applied to ending inventory. To remember which costs stay and which costs go, you might remember the FIFO (first-in, first-out) costs are the ones released to cost of goods sold, and that means LIST (last-in, still-there) is the amount held as ending inventory. The **last-in, first-out (LIFO) method** releases the last costs into the cost of goods sold and holds the older costs as the ending inventory amount. LIFO (last-in, first-out) means FIST (first-in, still there). A middle ground is the average cost method which takes an average cost of the inventory items and applies those costs to cost of goods sold and ending inventory.

As long as prices are fairly constant, the methods will all yield essentially the same numbers. During times of price changes, however, the methods will yield different results which impact both the income statements of the companies (through cost of goods sold) and the balance sheets (due to inventory amounts). During inflationary periods, FIFO produces the highest ending inventory and the highest net income accompanied by lowest cost of goods sold. When prices fall, LIFO ending inventory and new income is highest with cost of goods sold lowest.

These results also impact ratio analyses. Obviously, a higher gross profit percentage will occur if cost of goods sold becomes lower with the opposite effect seen when cost of goods sold increases. Profit margin before income tax shows the impact when net income is increased or decreased due to the method chosen. Higher or lower inventory amounts will decrease or increase, respectively, the inventory turnover calculation.

LO 6: Compute inventories using different methods.

With a listing of beginning inventory and current period purchases, the person computing inventory and cost of goods sold follows specific rules in selecting the costs to assign to either ending inventory or cost of goods sold. FIFO requires that the earliest costs into the system be the ones released to cost of goods sold. The later costs remain to be counted as ending inventory. All inventory items must complete the accounting period in one place or the other. LIFO rules mean the costs released to cost of goods sold are the latest ones into the system; the earliest costs are held as ending inventory. The averaging method computation requires determination of total cost of goods available for sale (beginning inventory plus purchases) which is divided by the total units that have been available. This calculation yields an average unit cost. The average unit cost times units left in inventory provides the ending inventory amount while the average cost times the number of units sold gives the cost of goods sold.

LO 7: Evaluate disclosure requirements for external

Because companies have the freedom to select the inventory cost flow assumptions they want to use, the financial statement user must be provided with information on the methods utilized by each company. The fact that different methods yield differing results will mean that the company's choice impacts financial statements and ratio analysis. These differences are, therefore, important in the decisions being made by financial statement users and are a required part of the disclosures found in the footnotes to the financial statements.

CHAPTER GLOSSARY

Accelerated depreciation methods: methods of depreciation that record a large amount of depreciation expense in the early years of an asset's life and reduce that amount each year

Average cost method: an inventory cost flow assumption that assigns an average cost to the units of inventory on hand at the time of each sale

Book value (of an asset): historical cost minus accumulated depreciation

Cash equivalent: a marketable security maturing in 90 days or less with little or no risk of change in the value at maturity due to interest rate change

Double-declining-balance depreciation: an accelerated depreciation method that calculates depreciation expense at twice the straight-line rate applied to the beginning book value of the asset

First-in, first-out (FIFO) method: an inventory flow concept based on the assumption that the first units of inventory acquired are the first sold

Impairment: a permanent decline in the fair value of an asset below its book value

Last-in, first-out (LIFO) method: and inventory flow concept based on the assumption that the last goods acquired are the first ones sold

Lower of cost or market (LCM): the value shown on the balance sheet should be historical cost unless the market value is a lesser amount

Modified accelerated cost recovery system (MACRS): the accelerated depreciation method prescribed by IRS for business use for tax purposes

Net realizable value: the amount the firm expects ultimately to collect

Specific identification method: an inventory method that assigns the actual cost of the item sold

Straight-line depreciation: a method of depreciation that assumes an asset is used equally in each time period of its useful live

Trade creditors: providers of goods and services to a business who expect payment within normal trade terms for the industry, usually 30 and 60 days

PROBLEM APPLICATIONS:

Multiple Choice Questions:

For each of the following multiple choice questions, circle the letter of the BEST response.

1. How many of the following are valuation methods used in financial reporting?
   - historical cost
   - net realizable value
   - lower of cost or market
   - market value
   - present value
     - a. 2
     - b. 3
     - c. 4
     - d. 5

2. Historical cost is generally used for valuation because it is
   - a. Verifiable
   - b. Reliable
   - c. Consistent
   - d. Comparable

3. Depreciation
   - a. allocates the cost of an asset over its useful life
   - b. sets aside funds to replace the asset at the end of its useful life
   - c. establishes the market value of an asset during its useful life
   - d. determines an asset's residual value at the end of its useful life

4. If a company recently purchased some equipment and wanted to report the highest net income possible in that period, which of the following would management be most likely to do?
   - a. expense the cost of the equipment rather than report it as an asset
   - b. decrease the estimated salvage value of the asset when calculating depreciation expense
   - c. increase the estimated useful life of the asset when calculating depreciation expense
   - d. record no depreciation expense.

5. At the beginning of 2000, Otto's Bus Lines bought a bus for $80,000; the company expects the bus to last for 10 years at which time it is expected to have a residual value of $4,000. Assuming Otto's uses straight-line depreciation, what is the depreciation per year?
   a. $8,000.
   b. $8,400.
   c. $7,600.
   d. $16,000.

6. At the beginning of 2000, Otto's Bus Lines bought a bus for $80,000; the company expects the bus to last for 10 years at which time it is expected to have a residual value of $4,000. If Otto's Bus Lines sells the bus for $60,000 on December 31, 2002, what is the gain or loss on the sale assuming the company uses the straight-line method of depreciation?
   a. 10,400 Gain
   b. 4,800 Gain
   c. 2,800 Gain
   d. 2,800 Loss

7. The Bryers Company was recently formed and made the following inventory purchases to start operations:

Feb 1	150 units at a total cost of $780
Feb 10	200 units at a total cost of $1,170
Feb 15	200 units at a total cost of $1,260
Feb 28	150 units at a total cost of $990

   A physical count of inventory at the end of the month revealed that there were 250 units on hand. Using the FIFO inventory method, the cost of goods sold for February would be:
   a. $1,365
   b. $1,620
   c. $2,580
   d. $2,835

8. In a period of decreasing prices, which inventory cost flow assumption would result in the highest net income?
   a. FIFO
   b. Weighted Average
   c. Tax
   d. LIFO

9. The McNally Company reported accumulated depreciation of 5,000 on its 2000 balance sheet and accumulated depreciation of 25,000 on its 2001 balance sheet. If no assets were sold during 2001, how much depreciation expense did the company record in 2001 on its income statement?
   a. 5,000
   b. 20,000
   c. 25,000
   d. 30,000

10. A company purchased factory equipment for $100,000. The equipment is estimated to have a $10,000 salvage value at the end of its estimated 5-year useful life. If the company uses the double-declining-balance method of depreciation, the amount of annual depreciation recorded for the second year after purchase would be
   a. $21,600
   b. $24,000
   c. $36,000
   d. $40,000

True / False Questions:

1. Compared to straight line, double-declining depreciation will result in a lower depreciation expense in an asset's first year of service.
2. Accounts receivable are valued at net realizable value.
3. Bonds payable are valued at lower of cost or market.
4. Depreciation is used to determine market value of an asset.
5. The gain or loss on the sale of equipment is the difference between the proceeds from the sale and the historical cost of the equipment.
6. The average inventory method will result in cost of goods sold being lower than the LIFO inventory method.
7. Buildings and equipment are examples of long-lived assets that would be depreciated.
8. An asset's book value equals its original cost less depreciation expense.
9. Inventory is reported at the either its original cost or market value whichever is lower.
10. Inventory valuation methods impact both the balance sheet and the income statement.

Matching: Match each numbered term with its lettered definition)

_____	1 Straight-line depreciation	_____	6 Last-in, first-out (LIFO)
_____	2 Impairment	_____	7 Net realizable value
_____	Modified Accelerated Cost 3 Recovery System (MACRS)	_____	8 Specific identification
_____	4 Trade creditors	_____	Double-declining-balance 9 depreciation
_____	5 Average cost method	_____	10 First-in, first-out (FIFO)

A   an inventory flow assumption that the last units of inventory acquired are the first sold.

B   provide goods and services to a business and expect payment within normal trade terms for the industry, usually between 30 and 60 days.

C   an inventory flow concept based on the assumption that the first units of inventory acquired are the first sold

D   the depreciation amount is twice the straight-line rate applied to the beginning book value of the asset.

E   an inventory flow assumption that assigns an average cost to the units of inventory on hand at the time of each sale.

F   the amount the firm expects ultimately to collect from accounts receivable.

G   the depreciation amount is the same each year

H   the depreciation methods used for tax purposes

I   an inventory flow where the cost is based on the actual cost of the item sold.

J   a permanent decline in the fair value of an asset below its book value.

Exercises:

1. The Somersett Company purchased a new delivery vehicle for $80,000; the vehicle is expected to have a useful life of 10 years and has a residual value of $5,000. Calculate the yearly depreciation expense using the straight-line method.

2. Allied, Inc. purchased a new delivery vehicle for $20,000; the vehicle is expected to have a useful life of 5 years and has a residual value of $5,000. Calculate the yearly depreciation expense using the double-declining balance method.

3. Post & Company purchased a machine for $100,000; the company estimated that the machine would last for 10 years at which time it could be sold for $10,000. However, after 2 years of use, the company decided to sell the machine. Calculate the gain or loss the company would record if the machine were sold for $80,000 using (a) the straight-line method and (b) the double-declining balance method.

4. Apocalypse Music, Inc. buys and sells music discs of local artists. At the beginning of March, Apocalypse had 1,500 discs that cost $7 each. During March the company had the following purchases:

	# of Units	Cost per Unit
March 5	3,500	$8
March 13	5,500	$9
March 21	4,000	$9
March 26	1,500	$10

During March 13,500 CDs were sold. Calculate cost of goods sold and ending inventory assuming the company uses (a) FIFO inventory method and, (b) LIFO inventory method.

Use the information in Exercise 4 above to calculate cost of goods sold and ending inventory assuming the company uses the average inventory method.

Problem:

Allen and Company purchased manufacturing equipment at a total cost of $130,000; the equipment is expected to have a useful life of 6 years and a residual value of $10,000.

Required
1.   Prepare a depreciation schedule for the equipment assuming the company uses the straight-line method of depreciation.
2.   Discuss the income statement and balance sheet impacts of depreciation.
3.   Prepare a depreciation schedule for the equipment assuming the company uses the double-declining balance method of depreciation.
4.   Explain the difference between the amount of depreciation calculated in part a and part c.

SOLUTIONS

Multiple Choice:

1. E
2. E
3. A
4. C
5. E
6. D
7. C
8. D
9. B
10. B

True / False

1. False - Double-declining depreciation will result in a higher depreciation expense compared to straight-line depreciation in an asset's first year or service.
2. True
3. False – Bonds payable are valued at present value.
4. False - Depreciation is used to determine book value of an asset.
5. False - The gain or loss on the sale of equipment is the difference between the proceeds from the sale and the book value of the equipment.
6. False – The average inventory method will always results in cost of goods sold is between the LIFO and FIFO inventory methods.
7. True

8. False - an asset's book value equals its original cost less accumulated depreciation.
9. True
10. True

Matching:

1.	G
2.	J
3.	H
4.	B
5.	E
6.	A
7.	F
8.	I
9.	D
10.	C

ExerciseS:

1. The Somersett Company purchased a new delivery vehicle for $80,000; the vehicle is expected to have a useful life of 10 years and has a residual value of $5,000. Calculate the yearly depreciation expense using the straight-line method.

    Straight-line depreciation =   (80,000 - 5,000) / 10 = 7,500 per year

2.

	Double-declining balance	
Year 1	8,000	(1/5 x 2 x 20,000)
Year 2	4,800	(1/5 x 2 x 12,000)
Year 3	2,200	(1)
Year 4	0	
Year 5	0	
Total	15,000	

(1) Although the regular calculation indicates that 2,880 of depreciation should be taken (1/5 x 2 x 7,200), total depreciation cannot exceed historical cost less residual value so that amount should be adjusted to 2,200

3.

Depreciation

	Straight-line		Double-declining balance	
				(1/10 x 2 x
Year 1	9,000	(a)	20,000	100,000)
Year 2	9,000		16,000	(1/10 x 2 x 80,000)
Total	18,000		36,000	

(a)   (100,000 - 10,000) / 10

Gain or Loss on Sale

	Straight-line	Double-declining balance
Proceeds from sale	80,000	80,000
Machine cost	100,000	100,000
Accumulated depreciation	18,000	36,000
Book value	82,000	64,000
Gain or (Loss)	(2,000)	16,000

4.

(a) FIFO
Cost of Goods Sold

	# of Units	Cost per Unit	Total Cost
Beginning	1,500	$7	$10,500
5-Mar	3,500	$8	$28,000
13-Mar	5,500	$9	$49,500
21-Mar	3,000	$9	$27,000
	13,500		115,000

Ending Inventory

	# of Units	Cost per Unit	Total Cost
21-Mar	1,000	$9	$9,000
26-Mar	1,500	$10	$15,000
	2,500		$24,000

(b) LIFO
Cost of Goods
Sold

	# of Units	Cost per Unit	Total Cost
26-Mar	1,500	$10	$15,000
21-Mar	4,000	$9	$36,000
13-Mar	5,500	$9	$49,500
5-Mar	2,500	$8	$20,000
	13,500		120,500

Ending
Inventory

	# of Units	Cost per Unit	Total Cost
Beginning	1,500	$7	$10,500
5-Mar	1,000	$8	$8,000
	2,500		$18,500

5.

	# of Units	Cost per Unit	Total Cost
Beginning	1,500	$7	$10,500
5-Mar	3,500	$8	$28,000
13-Mar	5,500	$9	$49,500
21-Mar	4,000	$9	$36,000
26-Mar	1,500	$10	$15,000
	16,000		$139,000

Average cost per unit = $139,000 / 16,000 = 8.69

Cost of Goods Sold = 13,500 x 8.69 = 117,315

Ending Inventory = 2,500 x 8.69 = 21,725

Problem:

	Depreciation Expense	Accumulated Depreciation	Net Book Value
Year 1	20,000	20,000	110,000
Year 2	20,000	40,000	90,000
Year 3	20,000	60,000	70,000
Year 4	20,000	80,000	50,000
Year 5	20,000	100,000	30,000
Year 6	20,000	120,000	10,000

a. Depreciation expense appears on the income statement and reduces net income; whereas, accumulated depreciation appears on the balance sheet as a reduction to property and equipment.

b.

	Depreciation Expense	Accumulated Depreciation	Net Book Value
Year 1	43,333	43,333	86,667
Year 2	28,889	72,222	57,778
Year 3	19,259	91,481	38,519
Year 4	12,840	104,321	25,679
Year 5	8,560	112,881	17,119
Year 6	7,119	120,000	10,000

d. The double-declining balance method of depreciation recognizes more depreciation in the earlier years of an asset's useful life and less depreciation in the latter years of an asset's useful life as evidenced in the depreciation schedules above. As a result, net income would be higher at the beginning of an asset's useful life and lower near the end of an asset's useful life when the straight-line method is used as opposed to the double-declining balance method.

Chapter 13
External Reporting
for Public Companies

CHAPTER SUMMARY

Knowledge of the information contained in annual reports of companies and the meaning of that information provides a much-needed deterrent to stock market problems. The lack of understanding of the materials provided in an annual report may cause poor investment decisions, loss of money, and the inability to invest for profit. While no individual investors can overcome the problems of economic downturns, company problems, or dishonesty by management, knowledge of the information in the annual report will go a long way toward helping investors avoid becoming a part of the problems.

Both the annual 10-K forms and annual reports are public information which can be easily obtained by investors without any cost to them. The 10-K includes information on the business, specific information of a financial nature which impacts the financial statements, information on directors and officers of the company, and financial statements. The 10-K and the annual reports often contain much of the same information so that examination of one of the forms will generally provide a comprehensive view of the company.

LO 1: Determine the role of ethics in business reporting and the implications of the Sarbanes-Oxley Act of 2002.

The problem of unethical business practices has been a recurring issue in businesses. Any individual in a position of power has some ability to accumulate personal wealth at the expense of others' well-being. Recent ethical failures have been so dramatic that Enron, a huge energy trading company, took bankruptcy; WorldCom, now MCI, recorded more than $9 billion in false assets, and Arthur Andersen LLP, a widely respected accounting firm, collapsed. As a direct result of these failures, Congress passed the Sarbanes-Oxley Act which created the Public Company Accounting Oversight Board. This body has the task of overseeing public companies and their auditors.

The Sarbanes-Oxley Act places much more responsibility on the CEO and CFO of public companies for review of financial statements, for fair presentation of the financial statements, and for review and monitoring of the internal controls of the company. Any officer who benefits from incorrect financial statements must return any funds obtained in this way. At issue now is whether the Sarbanes-Oxley Act will actually promote improved ethics in public companies. The act also requires companies to adopt **a code of ethics** and to have at least one member of the audit committee be a person who is a **financial expert**.

The act may encourage auditors to emphasize more labor intensive examinations of financial statements to avoid shortcuts even though increased work might increase the cost of the audit. The SEC also has responsibility for increased monitoring of companies. The Sarbanes-Oxley Act, if seriously considered by companies and their clients, may well lead to more diligence in reporting and the review of the reporting. If it works as it should, the users of the financial statements will be the winners.

> **LO 2: Understand the information found in a typical annual report**

An annual report contains a fairly structured set of information. Most start with a **letter from the chairman, CEO, or president.** A brief **description of the business, promotional materials, and selected highlights** follow. The five-year selected financial data are followed by **Management's Discussion and Analysis,** management's opportunity to tell the company story with a positive slant. **The Independent Auditor's Report precedes the Statement of Earnings, Balance Sheet, Statement of Cash Flows, and Statement of Stockholders' Equity. The financial statement footnotes immediately follow the financial statements. The final portions of the annual report include segment information, disclosures about market risk, information on directors and officers, markets in which the company's securities are traded, market prices, dividends, and information on ordering a copy of the 10-K.**

The section on segments lends important information which is not otherwise available. Segment information provides insight into the parts of the company. As a whole, financial statements combine all parts of some very diverse groups. Information on the segments gives analysts the ability to compare parts of the company to other units or companies in the same basic type of business.

An additional section on risk disclosures provides required information on risks associated with the nature of the company's operations, use of estimates, prospects for financial statement impact of future events, and vulnerability of the company in specific areas. Some companies are inherently more vulnerable than others in specific areas. The company management must disclose such problem areas. Also, important estimates must be discussed. Financial statement users have the right to know of estimates which might prove extremely important in understanding a company's position. This disclosure gives analysts an opportunity to determine whether their assessment of the effect of estimates parallels the assessment of company management. Disclosure of concentrations of risk also allows analysts to compare their assessments with those of management. Risk factors are numerous and varied and will not necessarily be interpreted in the same manner by everyone. The best predictor generally has the best chance for success in investments.

> **LO 3: Gather information about a company and obtain an annual report.**

Some insight into the more complex items on companies' financial statements also helps the analyst in understanding the financial information. On the balance sheet, accounts appear for marketable securities which may be classified as **trading securities, and available-for-sale-securities.** These are investments made by the company to earn a return on otherwise-idle cash. Their classification as current or long-term indicates management's intent with regard to the length of time the investments will be held before sale. Other investments include **held-to-maturity** (debt) securities and **equity investments in other companies**. Both of these are long-term assets since management intends to hold them for an extended period of time. The investments in other companies may be held to influence the companies in some way. Influence does not imply control of the company. Controlling interests in other companies require that the controlled company's financial information be combined with the financial information of the owner. This combining is called consolidation.

Leased assets also may be presented in two ways. An **operating lease** is essentially a rental agreement. The company is simply using the asset which belongs to another company; this arrangement is like rental on a house or car. Operating leases do not appear on the balance sheet. **Capital leases**, on the other hand, do appear on the balance sheet as both assets and liabilities. These leases represent financing arrangement in which the company holding the asset is simply using the leasing company as a lender. Depreciation on capital lease assets appears on the income statement of the company.

An intangible asset on the balance sheet, **goodwill,** indicates an amount paid by the reporting company for another company it has acquired. The reporting company paid an amount greater than the fair market value of net assets for the company, and that excess is recorded as goodwill. Each company with goodwill on its balance sheet must evaluate each year to determine if the goodwill has declined; if so, it must be written down as an impairment loss on the income statement.

Deferred income taxes, which may appear as an asset account or a liability account, occur because differences exist in recognition points between the accounting measurement of income and the tax law measurement of income. If the taxes are paid in advance, the deferred income tax account appears as an asset; if the taxes will be owed in future years the account shows as a liability.

Concern for employees' future welfare has led many companies to adopt **pension and postretirement benefit plans.** The future obligations to employees appear as liabilities. In order for the company to be assured of having funds available for payment of these obligations, it must also invest funds to accumulate amounts needed for future payments. These accumulations are assets for the companies. Amounts for the current year are income statement items.

LO 5: Explain why recurring and nonrecurring items are presented separately on the income statement.

Investors and other users of financial statements employ the statements as a means of predicting future income. For this technique to work well, the items used in the prediction must be items which can reasonably be expected to recur in the future. One-time numbers included in the calculations would create erroneous expectations for the future. For this reason, companies provide income statement information in special categories to help the analyst segregate items which are expected to continue from those not expected to continue.

Income statements usually contain a line called "Operating income" or a similarly phrased item. At that point in the statements, recurring items—those useful for predictive purposes—end and nonrecurring items begin. Below the operating income line, the analyst finds results of operations which are outside the scope of the company's regular business operations. Included in this section of the income statement may be **special items.** These items are unusual or not likely to recur and, therefore, should be excluded from predictions of future income. They are not, however, special enough to be presented as special sections of the statement by themselves.

> **LO 6: Interpret the net of tax disclosure of extraordinary items, discontinued operations, and accounting changes on the income statement.**

Three other types of items are labeled as **nonrecurring items** and receive special treatment. These nonrecurring items must be presented in a unique manner. Since corporations must pay income taxes as a normal part of operations, the tax on normal items is computed and appears as a deduction on the income statement. According to tax laws, however, losses are deductible and gains are taxable whether they are recurring or nonrecurring. Some provision must be made, therefore, for the tax effect of these nonrecurring items. This problem's solution requires than the special, nonrecurring items be presented **net of tax.** If the nonrecurring item is a loss, deduction of the loss from other income would reduce the tax owed. Companies show this reduction in tax by subtracting the tax reduction from the amount of the loss, thereby enabling the company to subtract an amount of loss that has been reduced by the taxes saved. If the nonrecurring item is a gain, extra tax will be due. The extra tax reduces the amount of the gain companies can keep. Therefore, the extra tax reduces the gain and is shown as a reduction in the gain recognized. Whether the items are losses or gains, the **tax effect is subtracted** from the gross amount.

All companies must report the amount earned for each share of stock held by investors. This calculation, called the earnings per share, appears on the income statement. A special calculation is required if the company has **dilutive securities**. These securities may be debt or equity instruments, but they have the characteristic of being capable of being converted to common stock if the holder of the securities desires to make the trade. If the company includes such securities in its structure, the possibility of the conversion creates some risk for the common shareholder that the conversion will take some of the earnings away from current shareholders. The risk of such an event caused the accounting profession to require a special calculation of earnings per share to show the extent of the potential risk. In this computation, **called the diluted earnings per share**, the assumption of conversion causes an increase in the number of common shares outstanding by the amount available for conversion. The calculation provides a "worst case" scenario of earnings for the common shareholder.

> **LO 7: Discuss the importance of skepticism in using financial**

Ultimately, the responsibility for interpretation of the financial statement information lies with the investor. While the company has the responsibility for providing adequate and accurate information, it has no responsibility for the manner in which investors use that information. The users of the financial information must, therefore, be cautious and responsible. Included in such caution is **careful reading of the auditor's report, careful reading and analysis of the financial statements and the notes to those statements, review of sales trends of the company and its industry, examination of the company's debt load, and computation of ratios.** Good news must be evaluated as carefully as bad news.

CHAPTER GLOSSARY

Available for sale securities: debt and equity securities traded on organized exchanges that management may keep for an indefinite time

Audit committee: a subcommittee of the board of directors that hires and works with the independent auditor

Basic earnings per share: an EPS calculation based on conditions as they exist on the balance sheet date

Business component: a portion of an entity whose assets, results of operations, and activities can be clearly distinguished, physically and operationally, and for financial reporting purposes, from the other assets, results of operations, and activities of the entity

Capital lease: a lease that gives the lessee the primary incidents of ownership such that the substance of the transaction is an asset purchase financed by the long-term lease instrument

Concentrations of risk: a lack of diversification in customers, revenues, markets, suppliers, or customers' ability to pay, which increase the risk of failure because a particular group of companies fails to perform their part of contracts

Consolidated financial statements: the combined statements of two or more entities that comprise one economic entity as defined by the economic entity assumption

Controlling investment: an ownership interest greater than 50 percent of the outstanding stock which controls the decision-making process in the investee firm

Convertible securities: bonds payable or preferred stock that owners may, at their option, convert to common stock

Deferred income taxes: liabilities that arise because the tax laws in effect for any year often differ from GAAP, which dictate how the financial statement information is to be reported

Defined benefit pension plan: a pension plan that gives an employee a pension at retirement of a certain monthly or annual benefit

Defined contribution pension plan: A pension plan that sets aside current dollars in an individual retirement account for an employee to accumulate over time to give the employee a pension fund at retirement. The amount of the retirement benefits depends on the amount accumulated through investments

Derivative: a security that has value based on another security or transaction, such as an option

Diluted earnings per share: a calculation that indicates the potential impact of any issued dilutive securities on per share earnings

Dilutive securities: securities that will reduce the percentage of ownership of current stockholders

Discontinued operations: the results of operations for a component of the company sold and any gain or loss from the actual disposal of the business component that are reported as a nonrecurring event on the income statement

Extraordinary event: an event that is **both** unusual in nature and infrequent in occurrence for a specific entity

Goodwill: the excess paid for the assets of another entity over and above the fair market value of those assets

Held-to-maturity securities: investments in corporate or government bonds that management intends to hold until the bonds mature

Influential investment: represents an ownership interest sufficient to influence, but not control, the decision-making process of an investee firm

Marketable securities: government or corporate bonds and stocks of other corporations

Net of tax: the amount shown for a transaction that has been adjusted for any income tax effect

Nonrecurring event: an event that is both unusual in nature **and** is not expected to recur

Operating lease: a lease that gives the lessee control of an asset for only a portion of its useful life and is treated as an expense

Option: a contract to purchase something in the future at a guaranteed price

Postretirement benefits plan: a benefit plan for employees that continues to pay medical and life insurance benefits for retirees, their survivors, or both

Special items: events that are either unusual or not likely to recur which are disclosed separately in the operating expenses on the income statement

Trading securities: debt and equity securities traded on organized exchanges that management has intentions of selling within a very short time

PROBLEM APPLICATIONS

Multiple Choice Questions:

For each of the following multiple choice questions, circle the letter of the BEST response.

1. A required component of the annual report is a/an
   a. Disclosure of the CEO's salary and bonuses
   b. Report on corporate citizenship
   c. Auditor's analysis of business risk
   d. Brief description of the business

2. The Sarbanes-Oxley Act requires that the CEO and CFO certify that
   a. they have reviewed the internal controls for effectiveness
   b. the financial statements of the company are accurate to the extent they can determine their accuracy
   c. no extra bonuses have been paid to executive personnel.
   d. The decisions made on the basis of the financial statements are the responsibility of the user.

3. Financial analysts normally use which of the following for ratio or trend analysis
   a. Management's discussion and analysis of operating results
   b. Five-year selected financial data
   c. Notes to the financial statements
   d. Auditor's report

4. An auditor's report excludes an opinion on
   a. Management's discussion and analysis
   b. Notes to the financial statements
   c. Consolidated financial statements
   d. Promotional materials

5. A company must disclose information regarding significant risk associated with
   a. unforeseen future events.
   b. the nature of the company's operations.
   c. the general economy.
   d. the difficulty of finding qualified personnel.

6. Concentrations of risk can relate to
   a. customers
   b. expenses
   c. business decisions
   d. auditor selection

7. Trading securities
   a. are expected to be sold within a short period of time.
   b. are expected to be held for an indefinite period of time.
   c. represent an ownership interest sufficient to influence the investee firm.
   d. must be equity instruments.

8. Consolidated financial statements are issued when
   a. one company has the ability to influence the decision-making process of the investee firm
   b. one company owns greater than 50 percent of the outstanding stock of the investee firm
   c. one company has a minority interest in another company.
   d. one company owns the securities of another company that are classified as trading securities.

9. Some firms prefer to report a lease as an operating lease rather than a capital lease to
   a. keep the liability off the balance sheet.
   b. keep the rent expense off the income statement.
   c. avoid providing lease information to competitors.
   d. avoid the calculations necessary for capital leases.

10. Special items include
    a. discontinued operations.
    b. errors in financial statement information.
    c. an event that is unusual in nature for a specific entity.
    d. income tax payable

True / False Questions:

1. Form 10-K contains a discussion of the business, common equity and stockholder matters, information regarding director and executive compensation as well as financial statement schedules and reports.
2. The audit committee is responsible for performing audits of the company's financial results each year.
3. The Sarbanes-Oxley Act of 2002 requires the CEO and CFO of the company to personally certify each 10-K and 10-Q form.
4. Trading securities are debt and equity securities traded on organized exchanges that management may keep for an indefinite time period.
5. An influential investment indicates that the investor has an ownership interest greater than 50 percent of the outstanding stock and controls the decision-making process in the investee firm.
6. A capital lease gives the lessee the primary incidents of ownership such that the substance of the transaction is an asset purchase financed by the long-term lease obligation.
7. Goodwill is an intangible asset that exists in many businesses, but according to GAAP may only be recorded when it is purchased.
8. Deferred income taxes always represent a liability to the organization.
9. Special items are events that are either unusual or not likely to recur that are included in the operating expenses on the income statement.
10. Dilutive securities may reduce the percentage of ownership of current stockholders and include convertible securities and options.

External Reporting for Public Companies

Matching:
Match each numbered term with its lettered definition.

_____ 1 nonrecurring event   _____ 6 held-to-maturity

        defined contribution pension

_____ 2 plan   _____ 7 trading securities

_____ 3 defined benefit pension plan   _____ 8 discontinued operations

_____ 4 available-for-sale securities   _____ 9 convertible securities

_____ 5 extraordinary event   _____ 10 stock options

A   debt and equity securities traded on organized exchanges that management may keep for an indefinite time period.

B   potential future shares of stock that represent a dilutive threat to the shares owned by current stockholders.

C   a plan that sets aside current dollars in an individual retirement account for an employee to accumulate over time to give the employee a pension fund at retirement.

D   the results of operations for a component of the company sold and any gain or loss from the actual disposal of the business component that are reported as a nonrecurring event on the income statement.

E   an event that is both unusual in nature and infrequent in occurrence for a specific entity.

F   debt and equity securities traded on organized exchanges that management has intentions of selling within a very short period of time.

G   investments in corporate or government bonds that the management intends to hold until the bonds mature.

H   bonds payable or preferred stock that owners may, at their option, convert to common stock.

I   gives an employee a pension at retirement of a certain monthly or annual benefit.

J   an event that is both unusual in nature and is not expected to recur and include discontinued operations, extraordinary items and cumulative effect of changes in accounting principles.

220

Exercises:

1. Identify the elements of an annual report that are prepared by management including those that give management's perspective on the results of company operations.
2. Describe the risks usually faced by companies that would be discussed in the company's annual report.
3. Describe the items that should be carefully reviewed to ensure that financial statement users can evaluate a company's results without management's bias.
4. Describe the different classifications of leases and the implications of each.
5. Describe the different classifications of pension plans and the implications of each.
6. Identify sources that can be used to obtain annual reports of publicly traded companies.
7. Explain the "net of tax" requirement for nonrecurring items.

Problem:

1. Pick a company that you are interested in learning more about and obtain a copy of their latest annual report.

   a. Review the annual report
   b. Summarize the key points addressed in the letter to the stockholders.
   c. Describe the type of community projects or social causes in which the company participates.
   d. Describe the type of opinion rendered by the external auditors.
   e. Summarize management's perspective on the company's operations as discussed in the management's discussion and analysis section of the annual report.
   f. Summarize five of the financial statement footnotes in your own words.

SOLUTIONS

Multiple Choice Questions:

1.	D	6.	A
2.	A	7.	A
3.	B	8.	B
4.	A	9.	A
5.	B	10.	C

True / False:

1. True
2. False; the audit committee, a sub-committee of the board of directors which hires and works with the independent auditor who actually performs the audit of the company's financial results.
3. True
4. False; trading securities are debt and equity securities traded on organized exchanges that management has intentions of selling within a very short period of time. Available-for-Sale securities are debt and equity securities traded on organized exchanges that management may keep for an indefinite time period.
5. False; an influential investment represents an ownership interest sufficient to influence, but not control, the decision-making process of the investee firm. A controlling investment indicates that the investor has an ownership interest greater than 50 percent of the outstanding stock and controls the decision-making process in the investee firm.
6. True
7. True
8. False; deferred income taxes represent *either* an asset or a liability to the organization.
9. False; special items are events that are either unusual or not likely to recur and are disclosed separately in the operating expenses on the income statement.
10. True

Matching Questions:

1.   J
2.   C
3.   I
4.   A
5.   E
6.   G
7.   F
8.   D
9.   H
10.   B

Exercises:

1.   Management prepares all sections of the annual report except the letter from the external auditors. Management's perspective on the results of company operations can be found in the management's discussion and analysis section as well as the letter from the president or CEO of the company.

2.   A public company must make disclosures about four types of risk that might significantly affect amount reported on the current financial statements. Such disclosures describe the risk associated with the nature of operations, the use of estimates to prepare accrual financial statements, the use of certain estimates that upon occurrence of future events have a reasonable possibility of making a material change to the current statements within a short period of time, and vulnerability due to concentrations of customers, revenues, suppliers, or geographical area.

3.   Any annual report will contain a certain amount management bias or "spin" so look for the following:
   - An auditor's report containing any explanatory paragraphs, adverse opinion or refusal to express an opinion.
   - Any disparities between the CEO's letter to the stockholders and the Management Discussion and Analysis section of the annual report.
   - Sales or other trends that is significantly different from the industry.
   - Debt levels and cash flows for the past five to ten years.
   - The company's ratio trends compared to the industry averages.

4.   An operating lease gives the lessee control of an asset for only a portion of its useful life and is treated as rent expense. A capital lease gives the lessee the primary incidents of ownership such that the substance of the transaction is an asset purchase financed by the long-term lease obligation.

5.   A defined contribution pension plan, a plan that sets aside current dollars in an individual retirement account for an employee to accumulate over time to give the employee a pension fund at retirement. A defined benefit pension plan that gives an employee a pension at retirement of a certain monthly or annual benefit.

6.   Sources of annual reports include the company's web site, *The Wall Street Journal*, PRARS, as well as others.

7.   "Net of tax" means that the tax effect, whether it is a tax savings or a tax cost, is always subtracted from the gain or loss to which it refers. The calculation is applied to discontinued operations, extraordinary items, and cumulative effects of accounting changes.

Problem:

The responses to these questions will vary, depending on the company selected.

APPENDIX

WORK PAPERS

	General Journal				Page
Date	Description	Post Ref.	Debit	Credit

Date		Description	Post Ref.	Debit	Credit
		General Journal			Page

Date		Description	Post Ref.	Debit	Credit

General Journal   **Page**

Account Name					Account Number	
Date		Post			Balance	
	Description	Ref.	Debit	Credit	Debit	Credit

Account Name					Account Number	
Date		Post			Balance	
	Description	Ref.	Debit	Credit	Debit	Credit

Account Name					Account Number	
Date		Post			Balance	
	Description	Ref.	Debit	Credit	Debit	Credit

Account Name			Account Number			
Date		Post			Balance	
	Description	Ref.	Debit	Credit	Debit	Credit

Account Name			Account Number			
Date		Post			Balance	
	Description	Ref.	Debit	Credit	Debit	Credit

Account Name			Account Number			
Date		Post			Balance	
	Description	Ref.	Debit	Credit	Debit	Credit

Account Name			Account Number			
Date		Post			Balance	
	Description	Ref.	Debit	Credit	Debit	Credit

Account Name			Account Number			
Date		Post			Balance	
	Description	Ref.	Debit	Credit	Debit	Credit

Account Name			Account Number			
Date		Post			Balance	
	Description	Ref.	Debit	Credit	Debit	Credit

Account Name					Account Number		
Date		Post				Balance	
	Description	Ref.	Debit	Credit	Debit	Credit	

Account Name					Account Number		
Date		Post				Balance	
	Description	Ref.	Debit	Credit	Debit	Credit	

Account Name					Account Number		
Date		Post				Balance	
	Description	Ref.	Debit	Credit	Debit	Credit	

Account Name					Account Number		
Date		Post				Balance	
	Description	Ref.	Debit	Credit	Debit	Credit	

Account Name					Account Number 1		
Date		Post				Balance	
	Description	Ref.	Debit	Credit	Debit	Credit	

Account Name					Account Number		
Date		Post				Balance	
	Description	Ref.	Debit	Credit	Debit	Credit	

Account Name				Account Number			
Date		Post				Balance	
	Description	Ref.	Debit	Credit		Debit	Credit

Account Name				Account Number			
Date		Post				Balance	
	Description	Ref.	Debit	Credit		Debit	Credit

Account Name				Account Number			
Date		Post				Balance	
	Description	Ref.	Debit	Credit		Debit	Credit

Account Name				Account Number			
Date		Post				Balance	
	Description	Ref.	Debit	Credit		Debit	Credit

Account Name				Account Number			
Date		Post				Balance	
	Description	Ref.	Debit	Credit		Debit	Credit

Account Name				Account Number			
Date		Post				Balance	
	Description	Ref.	Debit	Credit		Debit	Credit

Appendix

Account Name					Account Number	214
Date		Post			Balance	
	Description	Ref.	Debit	Credit	Debit	Credit

Account Name					Account Number	
Date		Post			Balance	
	Description	Ref.	Debit	Credit	Debit	Credit

Account Name					Account Number	
Date		Post			Balance	
	Description	Ref.	Debit	Credit	Debit	Credit

Account Name					Account Number	
Date		Post			Balance	
	Description	Ref.	Debit	Credit	Debit	Credit

Account Name					Account Number	
Date		Post			Balance	
	Description	Ref.	Debit	Credit	Debit	Credit

Account Name					Account Number	
Date		Post			Balance	
	Description	Ref.	Debit	Credit	Debit	Credit

Account Name			Account Number			
Date		Post			Balance	
	Description	Ref.	Debit	Credit	Debit	Credit

Account Name			Account Number			
Date		Post			Balance	
	Description	Ref.	Debit	Credit	Debit	Credit

Account Name			Account Number			
Date		Post			Balance	
	Description	Ref.	Debit	Credit	Debit	Credit

Account Name Sal			Account Number			
Date		Post			Balance	
	Description	Ref.	Debit	Credit	Debit	Credit
					5,213	

Account Name			Account Number 420			
Date		Post			Balance	
	Description	Ref.	Debit	Credit	Debit	Credit

Date	Description	Post Ref.	Debit	Credit	Balance Debit	Balance Credit

Account Name   **Account Number**

Date	Description	Post Ref.	Debit	Credit	Balance Debit	Balance Credit

Account Name   **Account Number**

Date	Description	Post Ref.	Debit	Credit	Balance Debit	Balance Credit

Account Name   **Account Number**

Date	Description	Post Ref.	Debit	Credit	Balance Debit	Balance Credit

Account Name   **Account Number**

Date	Description	Post Ref.	Debit	Credit	Balance Debit	Balance Credit

Account Name			Account Number			
Date		Post			Balance	
	Description	Ref.	Debit	Credit	Debit	Credit

Account Name			Account Number			
Date		Post			Balance	
	Description	Ref.	Debit	Credit	Debit	Credit

Account Name			Account Number			
Date		Post			Balance	
	Description	Ref.	Debit	Credit	Debit	Credit

Account Name	Ins		Account Number			
Date		Post			Balance	
	Description	Ref.	Debit	Credit	Debit	Credit

Account Name			Account Number			
Date		Post			Balance	
	Description	Ref.	Debit	Credit	Debit	Credit

Account Name					Account Number		
Date		Post				Balance	
	Description	Ref.	Debit	Credit	Debit	Credit	

Account Name					Account Number		
Date		Post				Balance	
	Description	Ref.	Debit	Credit	Debit	Credit	

Account Name					Account Number	7	
Date		Post				Balance	
	Description	Ref.	Debit	Credit	Debit	Credit	

Account Name					Account Number		
Date		Post				Balance	
	Description	Ref.	Debit	Credit	Debit	Credit	

Account Name					Account Number		
Date		Post				Balance	
	Description	Ref.	Debit	Credit	Debit	Credit	

Account Name					Account Number		
Date		Post				Balance	
	Description	Ref.	Debit	Credit	Debit	Credit	

Account Name				Account Number		
Date		Post			Balance	
	Description	Ref.	Debit	Credit	Debit	Credit

Account Name				Account Number		
Date		Post			Balance	
	Description	Ref.	Debit	Credit	Debit	Credit

Account Name				Account Number		
Date		Post			Balance	
	Description	Ref.	Debit	Credit	Debit	Credit

Account Name				Account Number		
Date		Post			Balance	
	Description	Ref.	Debit	Credit	Debit	Credit
